MOUNTAINS
BEYOND
MOUNTAINS

Dr. Paul Farmer with Alcante Joseph,
age fifteen, in Cange, Haiti,
October 2001

MOUNTAINS BEYOND MOUNTAINS

THE QUEST OF DR. PAUL FARMER, A MAN WHO WOULD CURE THE WORLD

—◆—

BY TRACY KIDDER

WINNER OF THE PULITZER PRIZE

ADAPTED FOR YOUNG PEOPLE
BY MICHAEL FRENCH

➤ DELACORTE PRESS ➤

Text copyright © 2013 by Tracy Kidder
Jacket photograph copyright © 2013 by Ron Haviv/VII/Corbis

All rights reserved. Published in the United States by Delacorte Press, an imprint of
Random House Children's Books, a division of Random House, Inc., New York.
This work is based on *Mountains Beyond Mountains: The Quest of Dr. Paul Farmer,
a Man Who Would Cure the World,* copyright © 2003 by Tracy Kidder, published in
hardcover by Random House, an imprint of The Random House Publishing Group,
a division of Random House, Inc., New York, in 2003.

Delacorte Press is a registered trademark and the colophon is a trademark of
Random House, Inc.

Frontispiece photograph courtesy of Moupali Das-Douglas, M.D.

Visit us on the Web! randomhouse.com/kids

Educators and librarians, for a variety of teaching tools, visit us at
RHTeachersLibrarians.com

Library of Congress Cataloging-in-Publication Data
Kidder, Tracy.
Mountains beyond mountains : the quest of Dr. Paul Farmer, a man who would cure
the world / by Tracy Kidder ; adapted for young people by Michael French.
p. cm.
Audience: 12 and up.
ISBN 978-0-385-74318-1 (hardcover trade) — ISBN 978-0-375-99099-1 (lib. bdg.)
ISBN 978-0-307-98088-5 (ebook)
1. Farmer, Paul, 1959—Juvenile literature. 2. Physicians—Biography—Juvenile
literature. 3. Missionaries, Medical—Biography—Juvenile literature. 4. Poor—Medical
care—Juvenile literature. 5. Right to health—Juvenile literature. 6. Human rights—
Juvenile literature. I. French, Michael. II. Title.
R154.F36K53 2013
610.92—dc23
[B]
2012024905

The text of this book is set in 12-point Tribute.
Book design by Angela Carlino

Printed in the United States of America

10 9 8 7 6 5 4 3 2 1

First Edition

FOR HENRY AND TIM KIDDER

CONTENTS

MOUNTAINS
BEYOND
MOUNTAINS

INTRODUCTION

MOUNTAINS BEYOND MOUNTAINS is a book about a remarkable man, Dr. Paul Farmer. I met him in Haiti, that desperately poor country just a two-hour plane ride from the American mainland. He was spending a large part of his time there, among some of the poorest of the poor, treating their illness and, more important, creating a public health and medical system for them. He seemed to be performing all this difficult work for no personal reward except the satisfaction of doing it. Dr. Farmer could have worked in any number of hospitals in the United States, conducting important research, curing patients, and living a comfortable and respected life. What made him do otherwise? I wrote this book because I was curious about him and I thought his life would make for a good story. I didn't write my book to make people believe in his cause. But well before the end of my research, I did believe.

I had been writing books and magazine articles for a number of years when I met Dr. Farmer. I was not the sort of journalist you see on television or in the movies. I didn't cover the news; I didn't put microphones in people's faces or go to press conferences. Instead, I wrote about life as it is lived out of the spotlight, by people who are not celebrities. I wrote a book about a team of engineers designing a computer, one about a schoolteacher, another about the building of a house, and even one about some very old people in a nursing home. I wrote about "ordinary people," but once I got to know them, I found that none were really ordinary. My most important technique for research was simply hanging out with my subjects. I would try to fit into their lives, to be as unobtrusive as possible, and I would try to understand them by watching what they did.

I hung out with Farmer, too. Although he was not famous when I met him, he was nobody's idea of an ordinary person. He was already an important figure in medicine, public health, and medical anthropology, and he worked impossible hours in impossible circumstances. In one of the poorest parts of Haiti, he had built a modern facility that provided health care for people who were living and dying in abject poverty. He seemed never to sleep. He seemed to be loved and admired not just by his patients but by practically everyone who knew him.

I spent long stretches with him in Haiti and traveled with him internationally. Traveling with Farmer is not like being a tourist. I accompanied him to Russia, a country I had never visited before. On my own, I would have enjoyed touring the Kremlin and certainly would have gone out of my way to see a performance of the Bolshoi Ballet in Moscow. Instead we went to Moscow's Central Prison, full of inmates ill and dying from tuberculosis, and then to an even more desperate outpost in Siberia. It was the same in Peru. Most Americans visiting there want to make the ascent to the ancient ruins of Machu Picchu. I would have liked that, too, but to travel with Farmer was to go directly into the tuberculosis-infected slums of Lima. None of this was much fun, to be honest. But it was spellbinding. And it was exhilarating to see how much Farmer and his small group of colleagues were able to accomplish, both in helping individual patients and in changing international health policies.

When you write about people in depth, you are always interested in how they grew up, what they were like as children. And usually you go looking for the evidence. For part of his boyhood Paul lived with his family in an old school bus, which they called the Bluebird Inn. After about five years of that, Farmer's father, a great big man who was nicknamed "Elbows" by people who played basketball with him, moved the whole family onto a half-homemade, fifty-foot-long boat that was moored in a bayou in South Florida. The family had little money, but most of them relished their unorthodox lifestyle, at least when they looked back on it. It seemed as if, for a lot of the time, they had a lot of fun. At one point Paul's father decided to earn his living as a fisherman, but he knew nothing about the ocean, or fishing. The experiment didn't last long. Soon the boat rarely left its place in the bayou.

Paul was a brainy boy and he did well in school, even though he didn't have a bedroom or a quiet place to do his homework. He went to Duke University on a full scholarship, and there discovered first wealth and then migrant farm workers toiling in the fields of North Carolina. Many were Haitian. He became interested in their lives because they seemed so different from the comfortable life he was leading at Duke, and so hidden from that lovely campus. He studied all things Haitian: the country's religion, its art and music, its language, and its amazing history. Haiti is a country created by former slaves, kidnapped West Africans who threw off their extremely cruel French masters—at times they had to fight the English, too—and created their own republic. It's the only place in the world where this happened, but it happened in 1804, when slavery still flourished here in the United States, and to make a very long and painful story short, Haitians have been punished ever since for claiming their freedom.

So Farmer imagined Haiti first, and then, after graduating from Duke, he made his first trip there. From that point on, he had a mission in life. By the time he got to medical school at Harvard, he was already working with friends to create the medical complex Zanmi Lasante, which is described in this book. Farmer's early life couldn't explain the man he became, but it was clear that he had learned something about poverty and how the world, when confronted with the poor, tends to look the other way.

Farmer is so gifted, so self-sacrificing, and so passionate about his cause that it is sometimes hard to believe he's for real. That was part of my problem as a writer—how to make him believable to people reading my book. That's why I chose to write about myself in this book—so that readers can see what it's like to meet someone who operates on a much different level from the rest of us. At first Paul Farmer made me feel inadequate and even a little guilty. He was doing all these wonderful things to end suffering in the world. What was I doing? But he didn't mean to make me feel that way, and I came to realize that he did not expect everyone to follow his path.

I hope that this young adult adaptation of *Mountains Beyond Mountains* will help a new generation to get a sense of the extent of global poverty and the challenges and opportunities it presents to those who want to help improve the world.

Farmer's life looked very difficult to me at first, and it still looks exhausting and endlessly demanding. But it is also a life that is rich in rewards. I remember talking about all this to my editor, who said something about Farmer that I think is true: "His life looks hard, but it also looks enviable. When he wakes up in the morning, he doesn't have all sorts of conflicting feelings about his life. He knows what he's going to do and he believes it's what he ought to do, what he was put on earth to do." If there is a lesson to this book, that may be it—not that everyone should go out and try to cure the world, but that all our lives are richer for having purpose, for pursuing something larger than ourselves.

TRACY KIDDER

Part I

DOKTÈ PAUL

CHAPTER 1

———◆—◆—◆———

I FIRST MET Paul Edward Farmer two weeks before Christmas 1994. I was in Haiti as a journalist, writing about the presence of twenty thousand American soldiers there. The soldiers' job was to reinstate the country's democratically elected government, in the process stripping power from the junta—a government composed of military leaders—whose corrupt and cruel reign had gone on for three years. The evening I met Farmer, I was sitting on a second-story balcony of a military outpost, talking with U.S. Army Special Forces Captain Jon Carroll. The compound was a desperate-looking place. Concrete walls enclosed a weed-dotted parade field, a jail, and a mustard-colored barracks. The captain was stationed with eight American soldiers in Haiti's rural central plateau, charged with keeping the peace for 150,000 Haitians, mostly peasants, spread over a thousand square miles.

The task seemed daunting if not impossible. The grisly murder of a popular local official—the assistant mayor had been beheaded and his body tossed in the Artibonite River—was making life even more complicated for Captain Carroll. The suspect most locals considered the killer was a member of the junta. He had been captured and briefly detained by the captain, only to be released by him for lack of physical evidence and reliable witnesses.

Carroll was shaking his head in frustration—about the crime and about all the challenges of peacekeeping—when an aide appeared and told him an American was waiting at the compound gate to see him.

There were in fact five visitors, four of them Haitian, but my gaze lingered on a tall, lanky white man in his midthirties as the group joined us on the balcony. The American introduced himself as Paul Farmer, a doctor who worked in a hospital in a nearby town called Mirebalais, helping poor people. Farmer had short black hair and a high waist and thin, long arms. His nose came almost to a point, upon which rested a pair of rimless glasses. Despite his pale and even delicate appearance, especially compared to the tanned and muscular Special Forces captain, there was something undeniably confident, even cocky, about him.

Farmer asked the captain if anyone in the compound needed medical attention. Carroll advised him that he had some sick prisoners the local hospital refused to treat, so he had ended up buying the medicine himself.

Farmer flashed a smile. "You'll spend less time in purgatory," he replied. Then he asked, "Who cut off the head of the assistant mayor?"

The conversation between the captain and the doctor went in circles. Carroll insisted he couldn't be sure, but Farmer said that everyone in the region had a very clear idea who the killer was. I sensed that the doctor knew Haiti far better than the captain, and that he was trying to give him some important information. He suggested the murder suspect be arrested again, and this time held indefinitely. This was the practical thing to do, he hinted, to imprison the man rather than risk the anger of Haitians who were starting to lose confidence in Captain Carroll's leadership. Farmer seemed to care less about the notion that someone should be considered innocent until proven guilty than about preserving a thin-edged calm in a jittery country. I found the two men's views ironic. The captain, who described himself as "a redneck," was arguing for due process. Farmer, who championed human rights and clearly was on the side of the poor, was arguing against it.

The captain couldn't hide his overall pessimism. No matter what he did or didn't do about the murder suspect, he said, nothing was going to change Haiti in the long term.

The United States Army had ventured here before, in the early twentieth century, to restore order during another period of turmoil, only to leave and watch from a distance as the new government eventually collapsed. The same thing was going to happen when the army left this time, he predicted. Haiti would always be a desperately poor, corrupt, broken society. No one could fix it.

Farmer agreed with some of the captain's points. Poverty and corruption were everywhere in Haiti, and the doctor had always been vocal about it. He thought the American government's plan to stabilize the local economy might help the wealthy business class, but it would do nothing to ease the suffering of the vast majority of people. Haiti occupies the western third of the island of Hispaniola, in the Caribbean, while the more prosperous Dominican Republic, once ruled by Spain, governs the eastern two-thirds. Each country has a population of about ten million, which means that life is far more crowded in Haiti. In fact, Haiti is the poorest country in the Western Hemisphere. Workers in rural areas, which are home to two-thirds of the population, earn less than a dollar a day on average. Health care, education, and food security are sometimes nonexistent in the central plateau. In 1994, 25 percent of all Haitians who lived there died before they reached the age of forty.

Doktè Paul, as his Haitian friends called him, made it clear that he didn't hold the captain or his men responsible for not being able to fix Haiti's problems; he blamed United States foreign policy for being naive. He insisted that imposing political order on Haiti, no matter how much financial aid was provided, wouldn't improve the problems of poverty and disease. These have their roots in the mid-eighteenth century, when the French government, which had claimed Haiti as its own, made Port-au-Prince, the capital, a major hub of slave trading. Most Haitians, who trace their ancestry to West Africa, have been exploited for 250 years, no matter what government was in power. First they were enslaved by their French masters. When they were finally freed, after a series of slave rebellions, their new masters were poverty, illiteracy, and lack of economic opportunity.

While the captain had good reason to be frustrated, Farmer, describing the work he was doing at Mirebalais, was saying something different. Even in a remote, understaffed, and underequipped hospital, if he did his best, a simple country doctor could improve the quality of life in Haiti. Of course, something told me that Farmer was more than a simple country doctor. Shaking the captain's hand and offering an apology for what might have seemed like a lecture, he disappeared into the evening shadows. As his group departed, I noticed that he spoke fluent Creole, the local language, with his Haitian friends.

For the next few weeks I stuck with Captain Carroll and other military personnel, continuing to write my story, more sympathetic than Farmer had been to their mission of nation building. Like Farmer, the captain and his troops were giving their best effort. I might have forgotten my evening with Paul Farmer had he not appeared on the same flight with me from Port-au-Prince to Miami. We ended up sitting together, dissecting our evening with Captain Carroll and the fragile peace that had settled over Haiti. Farmer seemed to know everything about a country that baffled me on many levels, and his insights helped me with the article I was writing. As he opened up a little, I found his personal life equally interesting.

Farmer had graduated from Harvard Medical School and completed his residency in internal medicine there. He had gone on to do a fellowship in infectious diseases. Somehow he'd also made time at Harvard to earn a PhD in anthropology. For four months of the year he attended to patients in Boston at the Brigham and Women's Hospital, and lived as a bachelor in a grubby church rectory in a poor neighborhood called Roxbury. For the other eight months he returned to the central plateau of Haiti, doctoring impoverished patients, many of whom had lost their land to a government hydroelectric dam project. He refused to take a salary for his work there. During the rule of the junta, he had been expelled from the country for his political views. Rather than stay safely away, Farmer bribed his way back in, to continue his work at the Mirebalais hospital.

My curiosity was piqued by his unusual life, and once back in the States, we kept in touch via email. A month later we hooked up in Boston, at a fancy restaurant with cloth napkins and good wine, which Farmer seemed to thoroughly enjoy. He struck me as incredibly happy with his life. I tried to understand how a Harvard-trained MD who could have enjoyed a successful, full-time private practice and a comfortable home in a Boston suburb preferred to spend most of his life with the forgotten poor. At one point I was sure he knew what I was thinking, as if others had asked him the same question. "I don't know why everybody isn't excited about it," he suddenly responded, meaning his work in Haiti. He smiled, a glow lighting his face. That moment, if not the whole evening, affected me quite strongly, like a welcome gladly given, one you didn't have to earn.

But after our dinner I found myself keeping a distance from Paul Farmer, mainly, I came to realize, because his optimism and happiness made me slightly uneasy. I wondered how anyone could give himself so selflessly to a forsaken land, refusing to be defeated by the considerable odds against him. Having finished my article on Haiti, I had come to share Captain Carroll's pessimism. Haiti's problems were impossibly deep and tangled. No one could solve them, including Farmer. Besides, the world was full of miserable places just like the central plateau, all of them hopeless. Most of my friends preferred not to think about the problems in developing countries, or if they did, they sent money.

Over the next five years I mailed small amounts to the

charity that supported Farmer's hospital near Mirebalais. He faithfully sent back handwritten thank-you notes. I wondered where he found the time. I was aware from media coverage that in addition to his work in Haiti and seeing patients in Boston, Farmer had begun working internationally in the field of tuberculosis. He traveled extensively, grabbed naps in airports, and, usually managing to find a computer, stayed in touch with old friends while making new ones. A very busy, determined man, running on high energy and idealism.

Perhaps my curiosity about Farmer had never gone away, and now I was more intrigued than ever. I wrote to him in Boston proposing that I write a magazine piece about him and his work. In December of 1999, we were together again.

CHAPTER 2

MY APPOINTMENT WITH Farmer was at the Brigham and Women's Hospital, a teaching affiliate of Harvard. The Brigham was part of a "medical mall" that included a teaching hospital, a full-service hospital, secondary-care facilities, and numerous physicians in private practice. The campus was impressive for what happened within its walls: chest crackings, organ transplants, molecular imagings, genetic probes, and virtually any other medical service known in the advanced world. With its distinguished reputation, this was where other hospitals in the country sent their most difficult cases, including people dealing with cancer, serious burns, psychiatric conditions, and infectious diseases. I joined Farmer on the Brigham's radiology floor, in a quiet room where he was discussing various patients with younger doctors, mostly residents, who were his students. Farmer was now forty years old. His hairline had receded slightly, and he looked thinner than I remembered him. Today he was dressed appropriately for an important Boston physician, in a black suit and necktie, and as usual wore his rimless glasses.

He still spent most of his time in Haiti, but as an attending specialist on the Brigham's senior staff, he was sought after frequently for his diagnoses of ID—infectious diseases. Farmer had become a recognized expert in the field, in good part because of his experiences in Haiti's central plateau, where he treated HIV (human immunodeficiency virus), AIDS (acquired immunodeficiency syndrome), malaria, tuberculosis, hepatitis, and cholera. He had written scholarly articles on the history of various diseases, often focusing on their connection to poverty.

Farmer suddenly interrupted a discussion with his students by picking up a ringing phone. "HIV Central. How can we help you?" he chimed.

"Worm lady!" he exclaimed after a moment. "How are you, pumpkin? . . . Oh, I'm fine."

The female doctor on the other end was a parasitologist, someone who studies how parasites, such as worms, invade and damage the body. She was a longtime colleague of Farmer's, and she had questions about treating someone with hydrocephalus—an abnormal amount of fluid in the brain's ventricles, or cavities—caused by a parasite. She asked if Farmer thought more tests would be appropriate.

"Listen, it's scandalous to say, but we don't agree. We want to treat his ass. ID says treat. Love, ID."

He hung up, his face glowing again. Farmer's whimsical tone didn't mean that everything he said wasn't completely serious. He wanted the doctor to begin treatment immediately, rather than subject the patient to further tests. He was having a very good time, as usual, and his students smiled back at him in approval. He seemed to enjoy the attention.

Farmer and his team had focused on six cases that afternoon, each something of a puzzle. He had methodically worked his way through all of them, step by step. A female resident on the team brought up the final case of the day, a thirty-five-year-old man (I'll call him Joe) who was HIV-positive, smoked a pack of cigarettes and consumed half a gallon of vodka daily, used cocaine, and just recently had overdosed on heroin. He had lost twenty-six pounds over the previous few months and had a chronic cough accompanied by chest pain. An X-ray revealed a shadow on his lung.

Certainly Joe was a likely target for tuberculosis, Farmer agreed with the resident. Of all the infections that can come crowding into a person with HIV, TB was the most common worldwide. It was rare in the United States, however, even in the jails, in the homeless shelters, and under the bridges that Joe often called home. Also, he didn't experience the fever, chills, and night sweats that usually accompanied TB. The resident offered that she liked Joe. "He's a nice guy," she said.

Farmer said, "Let's go see the X-ray, shall we?"

Less than a minute after studying the film, he seemed convinced this was not TB. He headed with his team upstairs to see the patient.

Farmer's long-legged strides might have carried him to Joe's room with reasonable speed, but he stopped frequently to give or receive hugs from hospital staff, exchange quips in Creole with a Haitian janitor, and answer his beeper to discuss someone's blood pressure, heart condition, or diabetes. Finally he led his team to Joe's door while he sang in creative German, "We are the world. We are *das Welt*."

Joe was isolated in a special room with negative airflow, just in case he did have TB, which can spread in the air and is highly contagious. He lay on his bed dressed in blue jeans and a T-shirt, a small man with scarred and wiry arms and prominent collarbones. He had an unkempt beard and unruly hair. Introducing himself, Farmer sat at the head of Joe's bed, folding himself around the patient in an agile way that made me think of a grasshopper. For a moment, I thought Farmer might crawl into bed with him. Instead, he placed a hand on Joe's shoulder and stroked it. Farmer had a way making almost anyone feel immediately comfortable in his presence.

He asked Joe a series of questions, listening carefully to his answers, all the while peering down at the man, pale blue eyes behind little round lenses.

"Your X-ray looks good. I think it's probably pneumonia. A little bit of pneumonia," said Farmer. "Let me ask you, how's your stomach?" He asked if Joe suffered from gastritis, or inflammation of the stomach lining.

"I'm eatin' everything in sight of me."

Farmer smiled. "You need to gain some weight, my friend."

"I didn't eat much when I was outside. I didn't eat much at all. Messin' around, doin' this, doin' that."

Just to be sure, Farmer asked Joe if he'd been exposed to anyone with TB. Joe said he didn't think so.

"I think we should make a recommendation that you not be isolated," Farmer replied. "We're ID, right? ID says hi. I don't think you need to have a negative airflow room and all that."

They kept talking, longer than necessary for a specialist whose job was essentially to determine the problem, make small talk with the patient, and proceed with his rounds. Farmer remained perched on the bed. He explained that it was important for Joe to take his antiretroviral medicines faithfully so that his HIV wouldn't develop into full-blown AIDS. They talked about drugs and alcohol, too, and Farmer warned him against heroin.

"But really the worst ones are alcohol and cocaine," Farmer continued. "We were saying downstairs during rounds, we were kinda joking around, saying, 'Well, we should tell him to smoke more marijuana, because that doesn't hurt as much.'"

"If I smoke marijuana, I'll create an international incident."

Farmer blushed, as he often did. "Not in the hospital, Joe." The two laughed, looking at each other.

Farmer talked about Joe's HIV. "Your immune system's pretty good, you know. Workin' pretty well. That's why I'm a little worried that you're losing weight, you know. Because you're not losing weight on account of HIV, I bet. You're losing weight because you're not eating. Right?"

"Yeah, that's right."

"Yeah," Farmer said softly. The way he stared at Joe's face seemed both intent—as if there were no one else in the world—and also focused elsewhere. I thought in his mind he might be watching Joe from a high window, as Joe went about what are known in social work as the activities of daily living, which in his case would mean scoring some narcotics, then heading off to his favorite underpass for camping.

Another person entered the room, a medical student whom Farmer had invited to join him on rounds. The room was getting crowded.

"I feel kinda lonesome in this room!" Joe said, gazing around.

"That's true. And we're going to recommend that you

get out of this," said Farmer. "So here's my heavy question for you—"

"What you can do for me."

"Yeah!"

"I'd like to have an HIV home where I could go to sleep and eat, watch television, watch games. I'd like somewhere to go where I can drink a six-pack. And I don't drive everybody crazy, runnin' out the doors and everything."

"Yeah," said Farmer. "I can see your point." He pursed his lips. "So I'll tell you what. I'll look around. And you know, I don't think it's that crazy an idea at all, what you said."

Farmer and his team eventually left the room, but only after it was clear Joe had been comforted and Farmer had earned his trust. A few days later, friends of Farmer's found a homeless shelter for Joe, but of course the social workers had to remind Farmer that shelter rules forbade alcohol consumption. Just to keep his word, I suppose, Farmer still pleaded Joe's case, not expecting to win the argument.

On Christmas, Farmer spent part of the day visiting patients outside the hospital. He brought them all presents, including Joe—who got a six-pack of beer, disguised in wrapping paper.

Joe seemed glad to see him as well as the gift. As Farmer was leaving, he heard Joe say to another resident, just loudly enough to make Farmer wonder if Joe meant for him to overhear, "That guy's a saint."

It wasn't the first time Farmer had heard himself called that. When I asked him for his reaction, he replied, "I don't care how often people say, 'You're a saint.' It's not that I mind it. It's that it's inaccurate."

Then he added, "People call me a saint, and I think I have to work harder. Because a saint would be a great thing to be."

I felt another inner disturbance. It wasn't that I thought Farmer was being vain; rather, I felt I was in the presence of a different person from the one I had been chatting with a moment ago, someone whose ambitions I hadn't yet begun to fathom.

A week later, on New Year's Day 2000, Farmer was back in Haiti. He had sent me a copy of his latest book, *Infections and Inequalities,* which, in addition to examining the link between poverty and disease, took to task how developed nations such as the United States and those in Europe treated poor, essentially invisible countries such as Haiti. He accused certain governments, pharmaceutical companies, and public health policies of favoring the "maldistribution of medical technologies." That meant that rich countries got the best medical care while poor ones were neglected. Corporate profits and ever-expanding markets were major reasons for this, he wrote in his book. I was seeing a very angry Paul Farmer, who didn't seem much like the Paul Farmer who worked at the Brigham. This one was shouting on every page. I emailed to thank him for *Infections and Inequalities* and promised to read his earlier books.

"I'm reading your entire body of work," I wrote.

By email Farmer replied, "Ah, this is not my real body of work. To see that, you have to come to Haiti."

CHAPTER 3

FARMER SENT A driver in a sturdy four-wheel-drive pickup to retrieve me from the Port-au-Prince airport. I had been invited to visit his clinic in the central plateau, in the village of Cange, called Zanmi Lasante. That is Creole for Partners in Health, an organization Farmer and some supporters had created in Boston to raise funds for his work in Haiti. Incredibly, the thirty-five-mile trip to Cange on National Highway 3 took more than three hours. Some stretches of road resembled a dry riverbed; other places were strewn with boulders or eroded down to rough bedrock. I would later learn that Farmer had suffered a slipped disk in his back from taking this bruising journey countless times.

As we lurched along, I saw beggars whose clothes were so tattered that I thought they'd disintegrate; villages of primitive wood huts; young boys working with hoes to smooth out patches of deeply rutted road, then opening their hands in the hope of a reward from people like me; and wobbly trucks top-heavy with passengers, impatiently swerving past oxcarts and donkeys as dust plumed in the air. I wondered when was the last time the government had tried to improve National Highway 3, but I wondered even more about the visible desperation of everyday lives.

We didn't reach our destination until evening. Cange, with a population of about thirty thousand, might be described as the most impoverished, famished, and disease-ridden place in Haiti. The original village was submerged when a government dam was built in 1956. The residents immediately became squatters, scrambling up the steep hillsides to remake their homes and farms on land they didn't own. In 1962, a Haitian Anglican priest named Fritz Lafontant built a primary school for local children. Later he built a small hospital near Mirebalais. The rest of the world, however, didn't pay the central plateau much attention, even after the first case of AIDS here was diagnosed in 1986, and a dangerous epidemic followed.

In this baked, desolate, treeless landscape, scattered with small tin-roofed huts and dusty walking paths, we drove through a gate and onto smooth pavement. Caught in the sweep of our headlights, Zanmi Lasante appeared dramatically on a hill, like a mountainside fortress. I studied a complex of concrete buildings that were half covered with tropical greenery. I would discover that inside the complex, amid leafy trees and spacious walkways, were an ambulatory clinic and a women's clinic, a general hospital, two laboratories, a large Anglican church, a school, a kitchen that prepared meals for about two thousand people daily, and a brand-new building called the Thomas J. White Tuberculosis Center. Tiled floors, white walls, and paintings by Haitian artists made the interiors inviting. The staff included Haitian doctors, nurses, a number of aides, and community workers, about 150 in all. A large generator in the compound provided electricity, and there was running water.

The day after I arrived, starting at dawn and ending well into the evening, I followed Farmer on his rounds, for the first of many times. The general routine was always the same. The clinic treated hundreds of people every day, who came sometimes from great distances, by foot, on donkey, or on the overcrowded passenger trucks on Highway 3. Dressed in jeans and a T-shirt, strolling into the main courtyard, Farmer was inevitably greeted by a crowd beseeching him not just for medical help but personal favors, such as delivering a letter for them to the United States, or procuring a pair of reading glasses or nail clippers or a wristwatch or just food. It took an hour to maneuver through the courtyard as he arranged treatment for the most serious cases. Then he retreated to a small room above the kitchen, where, before formally seeing patients, he sent and received emails via a satellite phone.

A hundred thousand people lived in the dam catchment area, but up to a million peasant farmers, coming from far away, relied on the clinic. There were other hospitals in the region, but none was as well equipped or well managed, and each charged patients for medicines and supplies. The policy at Zanmi Lasante was that everyone had to pay a modest services fee, the equivalent of eighty American cents per visit, because Farmer had been advised by local doctors that *not* to charge would encourage patients to take advantage of him. It was Farmer's style not to openly argue with authority, but he usually found ways to get what he wanted. He was, after all, medical director of Zanmi Lasante, and thus had the authority to make changes to the official policy. He declared that every patient had to pay eighty cents, except for women, children, the truly poor, and anyone seriously ill. That meant just about everyone was excluded. And no one could be turned away.

I began to see Zanmi Lasante as nothing less than a miracle. In addition to starting the clinic, Farmer's organization had also raised funds to build schools, houses, and communal sanitation and water systems. By using seventy community health workers, Zanmi Lasante had vaccinated all the children in the area and greatly reduced local malnutrition and infant mortality. It had launched programs for women's literacy and for the prevention of AIDS, and reduced the rate of HIV transmission from mothers to babies to 4 percent—about half the current rate in the United States. In Haiti, TB still killed more adults than any other disease, but no one in the catchment area had died from it since 1988.

The money for these ambitious programs was funneled through Partners in Health (PIH), headquartered in Boston. The bills were modest by American standards. Most TB patients, for example, were treated in their huts by one of the clinic's health workers, and the entire cost was usually no more than $200 per patient. In the United States, equivalent treatment ran between $15,000 and $20,000 per patient. The entire Zanmi Lasante annual budget for all of its services was $1.5 million, half of that in the form of donated drugs. The rest came from individuals and small grants. The owner of Boston's largest commercial construction company, Tom White, for whom Zanmi Lasante's tuberculosis hospital had been named, had befriended Farmer from the start and ultimately gave several million dollars to PIH.

Farmer, too, contributed. He had been awarded a MacArthur Foundation "genius" grant in 1993 and received a tax-free gift of $220,000, which he used to create a special research arm of PIH called the Institute for Health and Social Justice. He earned about $125,000 from Harvard and the Brigham; out of that he paid his personal bills as well the mortgage on his mother's house, channeling any left-over funds to PIH. In Cange, Farmer lived in a small house, with a bathroom but no hot water, on a hill across from the clinic complex. His true luxuries were a fish pond and a garden, designed and built by himself, something he'd first done as a teenager. He told me he slept about four hours a night but later confessed, "I can't sleep. There's always somebody not getting treatment. I can't stand that."

When I followed him around the clinic, hour by hour, he never seemed to rest. If anything, he was energized by seeing as many patients as possible. His staff sometimes complained that patients who crowded the hallways were unruly, but Farmer ignored their complaints. "You can't sympathize with the staff too much," he told me, "or you risk not sympathizing with the patients." Farmer was trained as an internist and ID specialist, but he had studied other fields on his own, including obstetrics and gynecology, because the needs of his patients demanded it. Ulcers, glaucoma, gastritis, gangrene, cancer, broken limbs, malnutrition, and a host of infectious diseases—almost everything came through the doors of Zanmi Lasante.

As many patients as he treated a day, he never rushed the process. As with Joe and others at the Brigham, every patient had to know how important he or she was. At Zanmi Lasante, he called older women "mother" and older men "father." He joked with pregnant women and gave small toys to children. The feelings of respect and sympathy were repaid. Many patients brought Doktè Paul a pig or a chicken as a present, had their photos taken with him, or wrote him thank-you notes.

The busier he was and the more patients he could see, I observed, the happier he was.

That impression was reinforced whenever I retreated to his office. On the wall behind his desk he taped sheets of yellow legal paper, on every line a task to be completed, and beside each of those was a hand-drawn box, or *bwat,* to check when the task was done. He liked knowing that every day he accomplished as much as he possible. New tasks—small and large, medical and personal—and their *bwat*s were added throughout the day. Rarely did it happen that everything was checked before he went home late at night, after making his final rounds through the clinic and TB hospital.

One afternoon I noticed the words "sorcery consult" on one of his yellow sheets. Around Cange people whispered that it was obvious Farmer had the gift of healing, but they added, "Doktè Paul works with both hands"—that is, both with medical science and with the magic of sorcery. It was ridiculous to think he could perform sorcery, Farmer said, but almost every Haitian believed in its powers because their culture had evolved in the absence of effective medicine. Sorcery, or black magic, was the Haitians' way of explaining suffering. Before there were clinics like Zanmi Lasante to teach people about germs and how to prevent or cure many diseases, people were sure that other people made them sick by putting a curse on them.

Farmer's sorcery consult was with an elderly woman who blamed one of her sons, angry and jealous of a brother, for "sending" a sickness that killed the sibling. As they sat in Farmer's office, she said she understood the clinic's message about germs and disease but still couldn't escape the conclusion that sorcery had played a hand in her dead son's fate. Farmer didn't tell her that sorcery didn't exist—it was too deeply embedded in the culture for him to dismiss it—but he assured her that her son had died of explainable medical causes. His words brought her some comfort, though he believed it would still take her some time to reconcile with her living son.

Farmer had a deeper explanation about sorcery, and he liked to engage me in conversations about it. He believed that the extreme scarcity of just about everything in Haiti, from food to clean water to clothes to shelter, created significant jealousies of anyone who had more than someone else. If you got sick, you might assume someone—even a friend—was jealous of your advantages and had put a curse on you. That was the mentality among peasant farmers, Farmer said. Economic inequality tore friends and families apart, as did simply the accusation that somebody wanted intentionally to hurt someone else.

"It's not enough that Haitians get destroyed by everything else," Farmer told me. "They also have an exquisite openness to being injured by words."

Farmer called sharing his insights into the country's culture and history "narrating Haiti." I think he expected me to agree wholeheartedly about the suffering of the Haitian poor and the injustices of the world, but I couldn't always summon the same anger he felt. I was, of course, sorry there was so much poverty and disease in Haiti, and I admired Farmer for his work, but I also felt that I couldn't be sorry enough to satisfy him. I'd end up annoyed at him for a time, in the way one gets annoyed at others when one has done them a disservice.

One afternoon, before I accompanied Farmer on his last rounds of the day, he sat across from a sad-faced young man named Ti Ofa, who was approaching the final stages of AIDS. He told Farmer he felt ashamed for having contracted the virus.

"Anybody can catch this. I told you that already," Farmer replied, opening a drawer to pull out some antiretroviral medication. He made Ti Ofa promise never to miss a dose. There was the possibility of slowing the virus enough to give him many more years of life, he told the patient.

It was the year 2000, and virtually no other doctor or clinic in Haiti was treating poor patients with the most sophisticated antiretroviral drugs available on the market. This cost Zanmi Lasante about five thousand dollars a year per patient—an unaffordable amount in the developing world—but Farmer looked for free samples where and whenever he could, mostly back at Harvard and the Brigham, even if it required begging on his part. Sometimes he received small grants specifically for AIDS treatment. He had begun a campaign to raise awareness of the need to stop AIDS in poor countries, where it was spreading like a brush fire. For every AIDS patient he saved at Zanmi Lasante, he lost maybe a dozen more. The epidemic was ongoing.

Farmer's final rounds took us to the clinic's main adult ward, then the Children's Pavilion, and finally the TB hospital up the hill. Visiting TB patients cheered him up because they were all recovering. He stopped at many beds, checking medications, smiling, and chatting with patients, who were always grateful to see him. Back at his house, sitting on a small patio lit by battery power, he set to work on speeches, grant proposals, and reading through a pile of clinical studies. A young member of Partners in Health, or PIH-er in Farmerspeak, was there to help him with the grant writing. The patio was small and cozy, like the cabin of a small boat at sea, I thought.

Before long that night, Farmer was summoned back to the hospital. A thirteen-year-old girl, moaning in pain, had arrived by donkey ambulance—a crude cart pulled by a donkey. Two young Haitian staff doctors hovered over her, not quite sure what to do.

"Doctors, doctors, what's going on with you?" Farmer asked plaintively, not angrily, as he examined the girl. He recognized the symptoms of some type of meningitis, an inflammation of the brain and spinal cord. But a spinal tap was required before a specific diagnosis could be made, he told me. Farmer did the spinal tap himself while the doctors held down the girl, who erupted with wild cries. *"Li fe-m mal, mwen grangou!"*

"She's crying, 'It hurts. I'm hungry.' Can you believe it?" Farmer said, and for a moment he was narrating Haiti again. "Only in Haiti would a child cry out that she's hungry during a spinal tap."

CHAPTER 4

THE MORE TIME I spent at Zanmi Lasante, talking with Farmer as well as staff and patients, the better I understood the challenge of treating the world's poor. Proper medical treatment couldn't be effective, Farmer believed, without serving a patient's other needs: basic education, habitable housing, clean water, food security, and hope for a better future. The clinic's seventy community health workers, who lived among the peasant farmers and had until recently been peasant farmers themselves, spoke often about the economic obstacles to treatment. They pointed out that the poorest patients tended to fare worst, in part because of malnutrition. "Giving people medicine for TB and not giving them food is like washing your hands and drying them in the dirt," went one Haitian saying. Others on Farmer's staff said that sorcery, not lack of food, was the primary culprit. Once they felt better but before they were properly cured, many patients stopped taking their pills, the staff said, because they believed, for example, that TB did not come from microbes but was sent to them by enemies, via sorcery.

In his early years in the country, while still enrolled at Harvard Medical School, Farmer himself had wondered about this, and devised a study that followed two groups of TB patients. Each group received free treatment, but one received other services as well, including regular visits from community health workers and small monthly cash allowances for food, child care, and transportation to Zanmi Lasante. What he eventually determined was that of those who received only free treatment for their TB, 48 percent were cured. In the group given cash and other services as well as medicine, 100 percent recovered.

Whether patients believed that TB came from sorcery or germs spread by coughing didn't seem to matter nearly as much as their material circumstances. The conclusion had surprised Farmer at first, but after he went back and talked to some of his patients—including a rather elderly woman who said to him with a smile, "Honey, are you incapable of complexity?"—he realized that a belief in sorcery can coexist with a belief in medicine, just as for many

Americans, himself included, faith in medicine can coexist with faith in prayer.

That study was for him a command to worry more about his patients' material needs than about their beliefs. Farmer decided that all TB patients in the catchment area should receive the full package of services, including the equivalent of five American dollars per month. The result was that no one at Zanmi Lasante had died of TB in the past twelve years.

One morning, I accompanied Farmer on a trip that I would soon learn was not unusual for him. A patient from Morne Michel, the most distant village in the Zanmi Lasante catchment area, had failed to appear at the clinic for his monthly TB checkup. Farmer didn't like the idea of "noncompliant" patients, those who did not follow his instructions. He wasn't angry or even disappointed with them—he accepted that all humans had weaknesses—but he was insistent that everybody take their medicine, even if that meant someone from the clinic tracking them down. Farmer had given himself that job today. As we readied to leave, one staff woman cried out, "Morne Michel? Polo, do you want to kill your *blan*?"

The woman was referring to me. The Creole word for "white person" was *blan*. The staff called Farmer a *blan*, too—*ti blan mwen,* "my little white guy"—which he found amusing and considered a term of endearment. It could also be confusing, as things were in Haiti. *Blan* didn't necessarily mean white-*skinned*. In fact, anyone who wasn't Haitian might be referred to as a *blan,* including the African American medical student who had recently joined the staff at Zanmi Lasante. With the woman's warning of hardship, I wondered what was ahead for me. Farmer drove us south in the pickup truck, down the rutted, dusty Highway 3. Soon a reservoir came into view, a mountain lake far below the road—tranquil blue waters set among steep, arid mountainsides.

I might have commented on the beauty of the sight had I not become accustomed to reading Farmer's face. He didn't speak at first, but his eyes betrayed emotion that jumped between disbelief and anger. We parked beside the rusted hulk of a small cement factory. A hundred yards away was a concrete buttress dam, which supplied hydroelectric power to Port-au-Prince. When he wasn't in Haiti, Farmer frequently gave speeches, lots of them, and invariably he mentioned the dam we were now staring at. When he discussed the interconnectedness of the rich and poor parts of the world, the dam was his favorite metaphor.

"If you looked at all this with peasant eyes," he said of the view in front of us, "the scene is violent and ugly."

The Péligre Dam, as it was called, had been planned by the Army Corps of Engineers and constructed in the mid-1950s, during the reign of one of Haiti's American-supported dictators. The U.S. Export-Import Bank had paid for it. The dam was a gift from the United States to the people of Haiti, but the only ones who benefited, Farmer said, were the wealthy Haitian elite and the foreign-owned assembly plants in Port-au-Prince that wanted inexpensive electricity. The dam stopped up Haiti's largest river, the Artibonite, and flooded some of the most fertile farmland in the central plateau. The flooded farmland was now a large reservoir or lake. Its tranquil beauty mocked the relative prosperity peasant families had enjoyed for centuries, before the dam was built.

With their valley and crops flooded, the farmers instantly became "the water refugees," forced to give up their land with little or no compensation from the government. They moved up the steep hills on either side of the new lake to rebuild their homes and replant their crops. The results were disastrous. Because of the steep grade, soil erosion from rain and wind whittled down food production year by year. Sometimes there were drought years.

Many families broke apart as the young fled to Port-au-Prince to make a living. There they cooked and cleaned and stitched Mickey Mouse dolls and baseballs, working twelve to fourteen hours a day. More than a few returned to villages such as Cange with HIV and AIDS. Families who remained behind to farm endured famine-like conditions and malnutrition. The spread of infectious diseases was inevitable, as were bitter arguments among old neighbors who fought over ownership of the land that was left.

I walked with Farmer across the top of the Péligre Dam

with its rusted railings and flaking concrete. To our right the choppy waters of the Artibonite rushed away, and to our left were a few small vessels plying the placid blue waters. Locals passing us smiled at Farmer and cheerfully said, *"Bonjou, Doc mwen"*—"Good morning, my Doc." Many waved—the lifted hand motionless, the fingers fluttering nonstop, like the legs of an insect on its back—and Farmer returned the gesture. "Do you see how Haitians wave? Don't you love it? You dig?" Farmer said. I enjoyed basking in his popularity and indeed wondered if there was anyone in the area who didn't know and like him.

On the other side of the dam, a path of loose dirt and stones veered almost straight up. Farmer began climbing and I followed. Eighteen years earlier, crossing a street in Cambridge, he had been hit by a car, and the surgically repaired leg canted out at a slight angle, making his gait a little awkward. He had his slipped disk to deal with as well, and suffered from high blood pressure and asthma. Still, he moved rapidly. When I finally reached the top of the hill, sweating and panting, Farmer was perched on a rock, writing a letter to an old friend. I couldn't see even signs of perspiration on him.

I was fourteen years older than Farmer but considered myself in decent physical shape. As we kept moving, however, I struggled to catch my breath and never stopped perspiring. The one-way trip to Morne Michel usually took Farmer two hours. I was clearly slowing him down, though he graciously made excuses for me. The houses we passed were more battered than many of those in Cange—dirt floors and roofs of banana fronds that leaked in the rainy season, turning floors to mud. How, I wondered, could anyone *not* get sick in those conditions?

Amid political graffiti scribbled in red paint on trees and rocks, we passed a group of women washing clothes in a gully. It was Saturday, wash day, Farmer said, but it was obvious that nothing was going to come out of the muddy water Maytag clean. Farmer insisted Haitians were a proper and hygiene-conscious people. It wasn't like they *wanted* to wear half-clean clothes, go without tissues or toilet paper, or apologize to their children for lack of food, he said.

"Misery," I commented.

Farmer used my word as a springboard for another narration of Haiti. "And don't think they don't know it," he said. "There's a WL line—the 'They're poor but they're happy,' line. They do have nice smiles and good senses of humor, but that's entirely different."

"WL" was Farmer's abbreviation for "white liberal," a group that donated quite generously to Partners in Health but which he now seemed to be claiming was naive. Days before he had told me how grateful he was for the support of whites, blacks, anyone who was prosperous—they all fell under his umbrella of WL—whether their motive was sacrifice, remorse, or even pity. His viewpoint had suddenly shifted a few degrees. "WLs think all the world's problems can be fixed without any cost to themselves. We don't believe that."

As we moved on, deeper and deeper into the mountains, I wondered what he meant. What additional cost did people have to pay in order to lift much of the world out of its poverty? Maybe it was a change in attitude, I thought, an acceptance that if something wasn't done soon, developing-world problems would become developed-world problems. Roughly one-third of the planet already lived in chronic poverty, according to United Nations statistics. Farmer pointed out that through the spread of disease, illiteracy, and consumption of resources by the poor, prosperous first-world countries would increasingly be affected—unless they scaled back on their own use of resources and brought education and health care to the poor. In his speeches, Farmer liked to talk about "the nation of humanity," as opposed to developed or undeveloped nations. He wanted everyone to see the interconnectedness of it all, and that the responsibility of the WLs was more than just giving money.

Three hours after we'd set out, we arrived at the hut of the noncompliant patient we'd been looking for. Farmer asked the young man if he disliked his TB medicines.

"Are you kidding?" he replied. "I wouldn't be here without them."

It turned out he'd been given confusing instructions on his last visit to the clinic, and he hadn't received his monthly five dollars. While he'd missed his last appointment, he'd continued taking his TB drugs. Farmer was relieved to hear it.

As we started our journey back, he answered a question that I would have asked sooner or later. "Some people would argue this wasn't worth a five-hour walk," he volunteered. "But you can never invest too much in making sure this stuff works." He admitted he needed to take occasional breaks from the intensity of the clinic, but mostly these time-consuming excursions were to set an example for the doctors and nurses who worked beside him. Nothing was more important than earning the confidence and trust of patients. It was a lesson Farmer had learned "on the ground," not in medical school. And he certainly hadn't learned it from studying public health policy, a topic that made him shake his head in disbelief.

"Bureaucrats," he would huff when discussing groups like the World Health Organization (WHO) or even a big-city hospital in a developed country. "We can spend sixty-eight thousand dollars per TB patient in New York City, but if you start giving watches or radios to patients here, suddenly the international health community jumps on you for creating *nonsustainable* projects. If a patient says, 'I really need a Bible or nail clippers,' well, for God's sake!"

Farmer had already pointed out how absurd it was that the United States had some of the best TB care in the world, but where, he asked, was the TB? It wasn't in the United States. It was in the developing world. The mind-set had to change, he argued to me, and doctors were the only advocates the poor had. Education, as vital as it was to Farmer and his cause, wasn't the only thing he thought the world needed. It was just the first step. I was beginning to see the extent of his ambition. He didn't just want to change Haiti at a grassroots level. He wanted to improve the lot of impoverished peoples across the world.

The way back from Morne Michel was only slightly less exhausting than the trip there. As I slipped and slid over the muddy ground, trying to keep up with Farmer, we came upon a clearing. Men in straw hats and ragged pants and shirts, with torn sneakers or flip-flops or leather shoes without laces, were gathered around a cockfighting pit. The two cocks, or roosters, were circling each other. Then one made a charge, wings flapping, and Farmer turned away.

He moved to the edge of some trees, where suddenly a couple of mismatched, beaten chairs appeared, courtesy of some nearby women. This always happened when I was traveling with Farmer in the countryside: one chair for Doktè Paul and one for his *blan*. I was grateful for the chance to sit and rest. Suddenly a dozen women surrounded us, old, young, and middle-aged. Farmer listened to their requests for an additional community health worker in their area, and I was sure he would find a way to oblige them. That was how things got changed for the better in the central plateau, one small but crucial decision at a time.

On the last leg back to Cange, I straggled up out of another ravine and as usual found Farmer waiting for me. I offered him a slightly moist Life Saver from my pocket, and he popped it in his mouth. "Pineapple, my favorite!" he said, as if the smallest thing could make him happy. Moving to the edge of a cliff, however, he stared somberly at the yellow mountains in front of us and the yellow mountains beyond those mountains and over Lac de Péligre.

The view reminded me of the Haitian proverb "Beyond mountains there are mountains," which meant that when you'd solved one problem, you couldn't rest because you had to go on and solve the next. The view of the Péligre Dam and its immense lake and the land it had drowned was, so to speak, another mountain to Farmer. It was a story of exploitation and disaster for at least a hundred thousand Haitians, and in one way or another, Farmer had to deal with it every day.

"To understand Russia, to understand Cuba, the Dominican Republic, Boston, identity politics, Sri Lanka, and Life Savers, you have to be on top of this hill," he announced in a light tone as we studied the view together. But there was a serious point to his words. The sight of the drowned farmland, the result of a dam that had made his patients some of the poorest on this earth, was Farmer's lens on the world. Look through it and you could see the billions of impoverished people in the world, and the many linked causes of their misery. I looked at him. He seemed to think I knew exactly what he meant, and I realized, with some irritation, that I didn't dare say anything just then, for fear of disappointing him.

Part II

THE TIN ROOFS
OF CANGE

CHAPTER 5

EVERY ADULT IS shaped by the experience of childhood and adolescence. I pieced together Farmer's youth by talking to his family members as well as to Farmer himself.

His parents came from western Massachusetts and married young. Paul, the second of six children—three boys and three girls—was born in 1959 in a struggling mill town. His mother, Ginny, a farmer's daughter, was tall and slender. She shared with her second child the same pointed nose and a tendency to blush easily. Ginny was patient, hardworking, and nonjudgmental. Paul senior, her husband, looked intimidating at six foot two and over 230 pounds. A talented and competitive athlete in school, known as Elbows to those who played basketball with him, he ran the Farmer household with a strict hand. His daughters affectionately referred to him as "the Warden" on account of his strictness—no makeup, no boyfriends, no staying out late. He was also a restless man preoccupied with making a living to support a growing family. In 1966, he left a steady sales job in Massachusetts and moved everyone to Birmingham, Alabama, because someone had told him, "Alabama is a sleeping giant."

The Warden found enough sales work to afford to rent a house in Birmingham, manage the bills, and keep his family happy. One of Ginny's joys was to have her first washing machine. To make vacations affordable, at public auction the Warden bought a bus that, oddly enough, had once been a mobile TB clinic, with a turret-like bulge in its roof to accommodate an X-ray machine. The bus's brand was Blue Bird, so the family called it the Blue Bird Inn.

Known as P.J. or Pel to his family, Farmer was a scrawny, energetic boy, intense in anger and affection, "with a huge brain," according to his sisters. Before long he discovered he had a photographic memory. Not much escaped his curiosity. In the fourth grade he started a herpetology club, for anyone interested in toads, frogs, snakes, and various other amphibians and reptiles. The first meeting was at his house, and when no one from school showed up, the Warden declared that all family members had to attend. A sister recalled that Farmer had put an incredible amount of work into his presentation, including charcoal drawings of reptiles and a lecture on various animals' diets and life spans. "We should just beat him up and go back out and play," the sister remembered thinking, but after a while everyone got interested and started asking him questions.

Parents of a friend in Farmer's advanced elementary school class introduced P.J. to Tolkien's trilogy, *The Lord of the Rings*. He read it in a couple of days and, after a conversation with the school librarian, moved on to Tolstoy's *War and Peace*, a thousand-page novel. He was eleven. "*War and Peace* is just like *Lord of the Rings*," he told his family enthusiastically. Years later he would comment that both books struck him as religious, in the sense that the characters were searching for an ultimate power and a meaning to life. Both of his grandmothers were devout Roman Catholic. P.J. liked going to Mass, serving as an altar boy for a time, but he didn't find in church doctrine the answers to the philosophical questions he was already sorting through in his mind. Church was nowhere near as intellectually satisfying as the books he was starting to read, he said.

In the late sixties the Warden quit his sales job and turned to teaching. But race riots, anti–Vietnam War demonstrations, and crime in general were on the rise in American cities, and Ginny and the Warden worried about their children's safety in Birmingham. So they packed everything they owned in the Blue Bird Inn and headed to a small Florida town called Brooksville, north of Tampa, on the Gulf Coast. The Warden had tried unsuccessfully to jam Ginny's washing machine into the already crowded bus. Farmer remembered the regret etched on his mother's soft face when they had to leave it behind, but as usual, she didn't complain. In Brooksville, short on funds, the Warden steered the Blue Bird Inn into a trailer park and declared this to be their new address.

For the next five years, using the trailer park's bathrooms and other public amenities, the Farmer family made the necessary adjustments that came with living in a bus. Ginny took a cashier's job at a Winn-Dixie supermarket and returned in the evenings to prepare dinner for everyone. Before the kids' bedtime, she read them novels such as *Cry, the Beloved Country*—about racial injustice in South Africa. In the morning everyone did chores and Ginny fixed breakfast before the six children hurried off to school. The Warden found a job teaching at a public school and worked a second job helping mentally impaired adults. When it was his turn to read novels out loud, he liked *The Swiss Family Robinson* and *Robinson Crusoe*, stories about people shipwrecked on islands and learning how to survive. He had a glint in his eye. Katy, Farmer's oldest sister, suspected that more family adventures lay ahead, whether everyone liked it or not.

Life on the bus alternated between moments of harmony and moments of chaos. In the turret, the Warden had built three bunks for the boys, with P.J.'s on top. There, P.J.

read scores of library books and did his homework. One of his brothers had a drum set, and the Warden okayed P.J.'s owning a large aquarium. Like sailors quartered on a battleship, they found privacy, space, and quiet hard to come by. But the eight of them managed, despite the occasional arguments.

When the Warden took everyone on vacations, exploring other cities and places, he and Ginny held forth on the geography, history, and cultures of the areas. The Warden had never quite figured out the vehicle's wiring, and whoever plugged the bus into a power source at a new campground often got a nasty electrical shock. "I did it last time!" the boys would argue. One rainy evening, the Blue Bird Inn skidded off the highway, plunged down an embankment, and flipped onto its roof. Miraculously, no one was hurt. The repairs took months, however, and with their home out of commission, everybody slept in tents. Whether the Warden intended it or not, hardship was part of life's lesson. When I asked Farmer if he felt deprived of anything in his childhood, he told me no, but admitted, "It *was* pretty strange."

Around the time P.J. entered high school, the Warden's appetite for more adventure took him to another auction. This time he purchased a Liberty launch, a fifty-foot-long empty boat hull with a hole in it. Katy regarded the whole matter as her worst fears coming true. The Warden had never gone to sea, but even in Alabama he had begun to buy boating magazines and kept them around like a reference library. He announced to everyone he was taking a year off from work to turn the Liberty launch into a seaworthy vessel. He named her *Lady Gin,* after his wife. Everyone was required to pitch in to build a cabin, where they would all live, on top of the hull. Halfway to a finished boat, money grew scarce, so the Warden came up with a plan. "We're going to pick citrus," he told his three boys.

P.J. said, "But, Dad, white people don't pick citrus."

"Yeah? I'll give you white people."

The grand scheme didn't last long because the pay was too little, but for P.J. this was a brief introduction to a world he would one day inhabit. Most of the workers up on ladders in the orange trees were Haitians. They spoke a strange language—Creole—that intrigued P.J. Before he got to know anyone, however, he and his brothers were ordered back to work on the *Lady Gin.* According to the Warden's latest plan, when finished the boat would serve as both their home and a source of revenue, through commercial fishing.

On its maiden launch, complete with fishing gear and a generator they could scarcely afford, the *Lady Gin,* with the Warden at the helm, steamed out into the Gulf of Mexico. One of Farmer's brothers, Jeff, later would say that he'd known all along their father didn't know much about navigation, no matter how many boating magazines the Warden had read. The first day out was fun for everyone as they swam and caught some fish, which Ginny cooked. But at night a storm rolled in, and while the novelty of a pitching boat at anchor entertained some of the children, Ginny and even the Warden grew nervous. In a panic, they tied a rope to the generator and threw it overboard, to serve as a second anchor. The next day, heading back to land, the Warden got lost, the hull grazed a rock, and the *Lady Gin* limped into port. There were several more trips out to sea, but almost none without something going wrong, and once, not following the channel marker buoys, the Warden ran the *Lady Gin* aground. Soon the boat was moored permanently in an otherwise uninhabited Gulf Coast bayou named Jenkins Creek.

Tied to a metal pipe in the bayou, surrounded by marsh grasses and lanky palm trees, the boat was the Farmers' new home. A gangplank led to land and the nearby Blue Bird Inn. The Warden attended yet another public auction and purchased two more vehicles. They were quickly named the Truck of Many Colors and Staff Car, the latter a battered olive drab army surplus sedan. The Staff Car made the kids cringe from embarrassment. On the way to school one morning, hunched down as if hoping to be invisible, P.J. asked the Warden to drop them off a block away. Instead, he drove right to the front of the school, honking the horn as he pulled up. "That'll show ya," he said.

The isolation of the bayou, while inconvenient, made the Warden feel safe from big-city dangers. He told everyone it was like they were living on their own island. P.J. particularly loved the ospreys that lived in a nearby nest, the otters that swam close to the boat, and the alligators he could hear barking under the clear, starry nights. With money from a part-time job in Brooksville, he bought materials for landscaping and for constructing a fish pond across from the gangplank. Never mind that his handiwork was in jeopardy when a high tide rushed in; if disaster struck, he would simply rebuild everything.

The Warden was happy with the family's new lifestyle, but Ginny struggled. If she thought life on a bus was cramped, a boat for eight, including teenage boys who were getting as big as their father, was a test even for a saint. She still didn't have a washing machine, forcing a drive to the Laundromat in town. Evenings, after a long day working at the Winn-Dixie, she restocked the boat's small refrigerator, fixed dinner, and washed dishes in the brackish water of the bayou. Drinking water came from a convenience store miles away—without permission, the Warden or one of the children quickly shoved their plastic jugs under an outside spigot and hoped no one saw them.

It was partly to avoid the unending houseboat chores assigned by their father that Farmer and his siblings threw themselves into Hernando High School's extracurricular activities. "No couch potatoes in the family," I once said to Farmer's mother. "No couch," Ginny replied. Farmer was very popular in school, especially among the girls, and he became president of his senior class. He was admitted to Duke on a full scholarship. Everyone expected him to get straight As his first semester, but for someone who had lived in a bus or on a boat for the last ten years, there were too many distractions. High culture captivated him. He became the drama and art critic for a student newspaper and wrote a review of the first play he ever attended.

The everyday world had surprises, too, like hot showers in the dorm. Farmer asked a fellow freshman, who was unpacking his dry-cleaned clothes, "How come you put your shirts in plastic?" Some students didn't even live on campus. Their parents rented condominiums for them. There were so many wealthy kids at Duke that Farmer was charmed by what money could buy, even if he had very little of it. He joined a fraternity and began dating girls from wealthy families. On one college break he returned home wearing a Lacoste shirt, telling the Warden that he couldn't wear clothes that weren't "preppy."

"Yeah, well," said the Warden, "Pel the preppy can still clean the bilge."

He did as his father asked. Farmer, like all of his siblings, craved the Warden's approval, according to Ginny. Unlike his brother Jeff, who excelled at sports, P.J. wasn't good at athletics. He tried playing baseball, but the only thing he hit with a bat was the head of the coach's son, by accident. In high school he pursued track, pushing himself so hard he'd throw up at the finish line, and played tennis.

When he came home from Hernando High with an A on a paper, the Warden asked him if anyone had gotten an A-plus. Years later, on an early trip to Haiti, an elated Farmer phoned to tell his parents he'd been accepted to Harvard Medical School. The Warden replied, "Oh yeah, we knew you'd get in." He had a hard time giving his kids compliments, as if afraid their heads would get too big, Jeff told me. What Farmer didn't know, Jeff added, was that the Warden bragged about P.J. constantly—his test scores, his full scholarship to Duke—but only when P.J. wasn't around.

In his last two years at Duke, for all his early infatuation with the social life and trappings of wealth, Farmer quit his fraternity and began concentrating on his studies. Focusing on science and pre-med courses, he earned mostly As. Ultimately he graduated from Duke summa cum laude. His father and his values had brought him back to earth. He'd come to admire the Warden's distaste for putting on airs and his fondness for underdogs, including the mentally impaired adults he had worked with and the trailer park neighbors who could barely make ends meet. Life was sometimes lived on the edge, yet for all the jeopardy the Warden unintentionally put everyone in, Farmer told me, in the end he always managed to rescue the situation. Once he focused on a goal, the Warden refused to quit. Nothing and no one could intimidate him. P.J. took on that behavior, too.

With P.J. away at Duke, the Warden continued to face

challenges. When the land next to Jenkins Creek was sold, he had to leave the bayou and sail the *Lady Gin* farther south, looking for another port. He accidentally beached the hull on a sandbar, and this time there was no easy way to free it. He dramatically told his teenage daughter Jennifer, who had accompanied him, that the best thing to do now was to give the *Lady Gin* a "Viking funeral." That meant burning the boat at sea. They collected everything of value, mostly books and photos, loaded them into the dinghy, which was named the *Mini Ginny,* and navigated to the nearest marina. When the Warden tried to buy gasoline for the Viking funeral, a man on the docks talked him out of the idea. "You'll kill yourselves," he predicted. *Lady Gin* was ultimately towed into port and its engine sold.

The Warden finally did burn the family boat, though, in a bonfire on land. That was one of the lowest moments in his life, Jennifer told me. Not only did it mark the end of the Warden's dream of going to sea and making a living as a commercial fisherman, it also coincided with most of his kids leaving the nest. He was suddenly without his usual cast of helpers, and he just seemed vulnerable, Jennifer said.

The Warden died in a pickup basketball game, presumably from a heart attack, when he was forty-nine. It was July 1984, and Farmer, twenty-five, was traveling between Harvard Medical School and Haiti. Returning to Florida for his father's funeral, he rummaged through the Blue

Bird Inn, discovering old books and letters. According to his steady girlfriend, who accompanied him home, Farmer was sitting behind the steering wheel, holding a letter that his father wrote to him when he started medical school. It said something like, "I just want you to know how proud I am." Farmer was sobbing.

CHAPTER 6

By HIS LATE teens, Farmer had acquired the ability to improvise and adapt, to make new friends, to focus on virtually any project in the midst of distractions, and—because the Warden could never be trusted to sit still—to view constant traveling as a normal existence. He had also learned to live without much privacy and with few luxuries. As a boy and then as a young teenager, he had entertained himself with what he considered life's essentials—his books, and the ideas and insights that constantly traveled through his active mind.

Yet his siblings, with the same parents and same unsettled childhoods, followed a more conventional path in adulthood. One sister became a commercial artist, another had a management role in a hospital's mental health program, and the third turned to motivational speaking. One brother was an electrician, and one, Jeff, became a professional wrestler (known to fans as Super J and to his family as the Gentle Giant). They settled down to a life of relative comfort.

"I never had a sense of hometown," Farmer told me. "It was 'This is my campground.' Then I got to the bottom of the barrel [Cange], and it was 'Oh, *this* is my hometown.'"

His intellectual growth came in part from his early travel abroad. In college he spent one summer and fall in France. Showing a natural resourcefulness, he had little money but got himself hired as an au pair, or domestic assistant, to a Franco-American family. On his days off, he went to political demonstrations, and in the evenings he attended classes in Paris, including one by the famous anthropologist Claude Lévi-Strauss. He returned to Duke able to read, write, and speak French fluently, and inspired to learn more not just about the sciences, in which he was naturally gifted, but about cultures and societies around the world.

As he resumed his studies, Farmer discovered the work of a little-known German physician, biologist, philosopher, anthropologist, and politician—a polymath—named Rudolf Virchow. Virchow had been dead for a hundred years, and only one full-length biography of him existed, of which Farmer read every page. Virchow made significant discoveries in oncology—the treatment of tumors—and parasitology, the scientific study of parasites. He coined more than fifty medical terms still in use today and defined a host of new diseases. He also campaigned for mandatory meat inspections in Germany, designed a sewer system for Berlin, and founded a nursing school and hospitals. Of particular interest to a brainy, idealistic youth such as Farmer, Virchow helped define the field of medical anthropology— the study of human health and disease and public health care systems. At age twenty-six, Virchow wrote passionately that terrible social conditions in an impoverished part of Germany called Upper Silesia were the cause of a malaria and dysentery epidemic. His recommendation to the German government: if it wanted to do something about the epidemic, it needed to end the malnutrition, overcrowding, and poor hygiene. Better yet, he added, allow for a full and unlimited democracy in Upper Silesia.

Virchow was the perfect role model for anyone who wanted to change the world, or at least lessen the inequality between the rich and poor. One of Farmer's favorite Virchow quotes was "The physicians are the natural attorneys of the poor, and the social problems should largely be solved by them." Virchow viewed the world in a way that made sense to Farmer, his vision a comprehensive one that included pathology—the study of disease—with social medicine, politics, and anthropology.

Farmer, about to graduate from Duke, found an equivalent to Upper Silesia not far from campus. He'd been following current events in Latin America, including the murder of Salvadoran archbishop Oscar Romero by a right-wing death squad. In addition to attending protests over the murder at the Duke Chapel, he began reading about a branch of Catholicism called "liberation theology," which Archbishop Romero had been preaching. The central doctrine of liberation theology was that the Catholic Church had an obligation to provide a "preferential option for the poor." Liberation theology meant that the Christian faith carried an obligation to promote social justice, and from its own resources the Church had a duty to help the poor wherever and whenever possible. The more he read, the more Farmer thought, "Wow! This ain't the Catholicism I remember."

Turning his back on the affluent trappings of Duke, Farmer began sensitizing himself to the centuries-old plight of the the poor. Oppression occurred, he saw, when governments and most people simply ignored the poor or, worse, abused them. At a migrant labor camp not far from Duke, Farmer met a Belgian nun, Julianna DeWolf, who worked with Friends of the United Farm Workers. Arrogant and humble at the same time, the radical, fearless nun and her fellow sisters were the most committed individuals Farmer had ever met. "They were just so much more militant, if that's the word, than the WLs and the academics.

They were standing up to the growers. They were the ones schlepping the workers to the clinics or court, translating for them, getting them groceries or driver's licenses."

In Sister Julianna's company, on tours of North Carolina tobacco plantations, Farmer met a number of Haitians. They were living in such wretched conditions that he wrote an article about the deplorable situation. He also began reading everything he could about Haiti, its history, language, music, literature, painting, and Voodoo religion. Haitians had a remarkable core culture, but it was buried under years of oppression and poverty. At home and abroad, he thought, Haitians were the underdogs of the underdogs, "the shafted of the shafted." He likened their plight, starting from their years of slavery under their French masters, to *The Lord of the Rings*—an ongoing story of the terrible struggle between the rich and the poor, between good and evil.

Farmer was particularly seduced by the Creole language, a blend of French and various African languages, unique to Haiti. It was lovely and expressive and born of grim necessity. The French masters had separated slaves who spoke the same African language, so in secret they had fashioned their own common tongue in order to communicate more effectively. Farmer began to study Creole before he went to Haiti in the spring of 1983. It would be his first trip there, and he planned to spend about a year before deciding which medical school to attend, Harvard or Case

Western. They were the only schools to offer a joint degree as a doctor-anthropologist. He hoped that Haiti would provide him field opportunities to integrate the two disciplines and to make sure this was the career he really wanted.

On arrival, Farmer didn't spend much time in Port-au-Prince. The country was run by the Duvaliers, a tyrannical family in power since 1957. When François Duvalier, known as "Papa Doc," died of a heart attack in 1971, his nineteen-year-old son, Jean-Claude Duvalier, took over the reins of power and became known as "Baby Doc." Wherever Farmer walked in the city he felt the presence of the *tontons macoutes,* Baby Doc's infamous secret police, who hid behind dark glasses and seemed to shadow foreign visitors. Farmer was also appalled by the extent of the city's slums. Because of contacts he'd made in the States with the Mellon family—wealthy heirs of Pittsburgh banker and philanthropist Andrew Mellon—he quickly headed to the town of Deschapelles, in the lower Artibonite Valley. The Mellon family had financed a hospital called Hospital Albert Schweitzer, named for the famous German theologian and physician who had worked as a doctor in West Africa. Farmer hoped to land a job at Schweitzer. He was disappointed to discover that the hospital was staffed mostly with white, foreign doctors, with little if any effort placed on training Haitian doctors to treat Haitians. He was also disappointed that no job openings existed, despite his contacts.

Farmer moved on, to the town of Mirebalais in Haiti's

central plateau, where he would eventually meet the Haitian Anglican priest Father Lafontant and discover just how poor the poor could be. He didn't know it at the time, but he was getting closer to his "hometown," Cange. Wherever he went in Haiti he carried a camera, a tape recorder, and a notebook. If he wanted to combine his love of medicine with anthropology, recording his observations, testing his academic theories, he thought, there was perhaps no better laboratory in the Western Hemisphere.

CHAPTER 7

---※ ⋅◂ ▸⋅ ※---

SETTLING IN THE small town of Mirebalais, Farmer found work with a charity called Eye Care Haiti, headquartered in Port-au-Prince, which conducted mobile "outreach clinics" in the countryside. Carrying his camera and tape recorder, he and others on the Eye Care team journeyed out in a Land Rover during the week, seeing patients, then returned to Port-au-Prince on weekends.

One afternoon in Mirebalais, an attractive eighteen-year-old British woman trudged through a light, warm rain, hoping to make a phone call to her father, who lived in Buckinghamshire, England. Her name was Ophelia Dahl. Her well-known father, the writer Roald Dahl, had sent her to Haiti for a taste of adventure and perhaps to find a useful life serving others. Ophelia had vague ideas about going into medicine one day, and for now she was working as a volunteer for Eye Care. After recently receiving a letter from her father, she was eager to talk to him about family matters. She quickly discovered that phone lines at the Teleco building weren't functioning. Ophelia wasn't surprised—the phones in Mirebalais worked half the time at best—but she still felt frustrated, and a little dejected.

Walking back to the Eye Care house, her gaze strayed to the building's balcony. She was surprised to see a "pale and rangy fellow," a *blan* like her, appearing totally at ease in a town where white people were not common. This man didn't look like a misplaced tourist or businessman. She began to feel resentment toward him without even knowing who he was. Ophelia had been living among Haitians for months, eating their food and doing her best to speak their language, and who was this new guy invading her turf? She debated what to do only for a moment. Like a proper, well-bred English girl, she marched inside and introduced herself to the new *blan* in town. He told her his name was Paul Farmer, from Florida, and he'd come to Haiti for his own anthropology work, among other things. She didn't know very much about anthropology, but the newcomer's friendliness put her at ease.

Minutes later, they were sitting across from each other at a small table in the building's common room. As they chatted about Haiti, at some point Farmer asked, "Tell me about your family." He not only knew how to make her comfortable, she saw, but gave the impression that he cared only about her at that moment. Before long she was telling this stranger about her anxiety in not being able to phone her father, and giving details of her family life, including about her famous mother, Patricia Neal, the actress. Her mom had suffered a stroke, and after enduring a long convalescence, then had to confront a painful divorce from Ophelia's father. Normally reserved, Ophelia didn't hold herself back with Farmer, showing him even her "outrageous side," with its off-color humor and occasional swearing. She liked the chance to be herself. She also liked that Farmer wasn't overly impressed with the celebrity of her parents. He told stories of his own eccentric upbringing, and these made her laugh. He had come to Eye Care hoping to join up with the doctors, he said. Ophelia gave him a rundown of the various personalities at the clinic. She wouldn't have liked him half so much if he hadn't said "Thank you for telling me that" with such evident feeling.

They talked until three in the morning. The next few days she joined Farmer and the medical team in the Land Rover. She'd been in the country for four months, while Farmer had just arrived, but he seemed to know far more about Haiti than Ophelia did. He was mastering Creole "like a rat," in the Haitian idiom, and he stopped to talk to peasants whenever he could, soaking up information.

Ophelia peppered him with questions, like why were so many people here hopelessly sick, and why weren't the roads better? He answered carefully, not wanting to reveal too much of himself, she thought, until he was sure who she was. At the same time, he was embarrassingly enthusiastic about all things Haiti, as if it were his adopted country. He gave her the Latin names of trees and shrubs that they passed. He waved and grinned at everyone—like a nerd, she thought. He didn't mind being called a *blan*. Here was someone she might be able to have fun with, but Ophelia also saw a sensitive, guarded side to Farmer. Once, when she made fun of his constant waving to peasants, she felt him close up on her, and she knew if she wanted to know him better, she should not make that mistake again.

At the end of that week, when Ophelia accompanied Farmer back to Port-au-Prince, the Rover came to an abrupt stop on the highway. Just ahead, a small, battered pickup truck lay on its side. Overturned baskets and mangoes were strewn all around. The passengers in the truck, called a *tap-tap*, had been market women in head wraps, and they now sat by the side of road looking dazed. There were policemen at the scene, hovering around the lifeless body of one of the passengers. For Ophelia, the scene would become a fixture in her memory. She wasn't the only one affected. She looked over at Paul as the Rover edged around the accident and on to Port-au-Prince. He had become, she would remember, "very, very silent."

Over the next month or so, Ophelia saw Farmer whenever she could, both in Mirebalais and Port-au-Prince, and they enjoyed each other's company. He called her "Min," and he was Pel or P.J. When he was in the city, he lived in an old ruin of a mansion on a garbage-littered lot. His second-story flat afforded a view of the harbor and, off to one side, the tents and cardboard huts of a slum. When Ophelia came to visit, Farmer was usually either reading or writing. One day he told her he had composed a poem called "The Mango Lady," based on the accident they'd witnessed, and dedicated it to Ophelia. She was moved as he read it aloud, seeing that Farmer was just as sensitive as she was to the fragility of Haitian life. That bond deepened their relationship, she felt. "The Mango Lady" to Farmer was an illustration that accidents didn't happen by accident. There was nothing accidental about a wretched road, or an overcrowded tap-tap with bad brakes, or the desperation of peasant women needing to sell something at market in order to feed their families that night.

While he had not yet attended Harvard Medical School, it seemed to Ophelia that Farmer already seemed to know a lot about medicine and especially anthropology. He said he'd come to Haiti to do ethnography—a branch of anthropology that centered on learning about a culture from the people who had inherited and were making culture—and his special field was going to be medical ethnography. Their five-year age difference made it easier for Ophelia to accept him as her teacher, but Farmer knew so much that age hardly mattered. On a daily basis he commented on Haitian poverty, history, and culture, as well as the long-standing American habit of lavishing aid on corrupt dictators such as Baby Doc Duvalier. He liked to talk about Graham Greene, the British novelist, and his novel on Haiti, *The Comedians,* which narrated the story of the Duvaliers and their secret police. If Farmer ever said anything cryptic and Ophelia challenged him, she noticed that he stopped being so forthcoming. Better just to say, she realized, "Tell me more," and he would clarify his point. She welcomed all of his insights. Before she'd met Farmer, Haiti had seemed merely vivid—terrible and strange much of the time. Farmer became a translator of her experiences. He put them in context of a comprehensive theory of poverty, of a world designed by the elites of all nations to serve their own ends, a design that ignored the basic human rights of the poor.

Discussing the future, when he told her that he wanted to "lend a voice to the voiceless," she understood his ambitions more clearly. He was going to be a doctor to poor people. Maybe he'd end up working in Africa or an American inner city, he said, but Ophelia was betting it would be Haiti. Farmer had not only exposed his deepest self to her, but also to some degree changed her life. Years later she would tell me, "I think there's a point when you realize the world has just been revealed to you. It's like realizing your parents are both good and bad. It's sort of, Oh no, things will never be quite the same again."

She was more than smitten by Farmer. She wondered if she was falling in love. But she had to return to England, where she hoped to start her pre-med work. She had told Pel she wanted to become a doctor, too.

"Great," he said earnestly. "You know what you should do? Make flash cards."

She left Pel several contemporary novels—literature discussions had been one of their bonds—and they promised to write each other.

Soon after she returned to England, her father took her to lunch with Graham Greene. The elderly novelist, tall and stooped, was genuinely glad for news of Haiti. He inscribed Ophelia's copy of *The Comedians*, "To Ophelia, who knows the real Haiti." If he really thought that of her, she wondered, what would he make of Paul Farmer?

CHAPTER 8

In late May 1983, soon after Ophelia returned to England, Farmer saw Cange for the first time. The Haitian priest Fritz Lafontant, whom Farmer had met in Mirebalais, was his guide. As they toured Cange in the priest's pickup, the treeless, dusty landscape struck Farmer as "amazingly, biblically dry and barren." Located half a mile from the Péligre Dam and reservoir, the town was little more than a squatter settlement for the water refugees.

The priest told Farmer stories of the dam, about the chaos and instability it had created almost overnight. The peasant farmers had watched the dam being built, but even when it began blocking the Artibonite River, forming a reservoir that flooded their farms, they felt stunned disbelief. The government had given them no clear warning. One of the old people remembered seeing the water rising and suddenly realizing that his house and goats would soon be underwater; he picked up a child and a goat and scrambled up the hill. Families everywhere hurried away, carrying whatever they could save of their former lives.

Maybe they had lost their homes, the peasants tried to console themselves, but at least they had their goats and their black, low-slung Creole pigs. To a Haitian, every pig was a bank account—it could be bartered for food, shelter, medicine, even school tuition for a child. In the early 1980s, however, afraid that an outbreak of African swine fever in neighboring Dominican Republic would spread over the entire island, the United States led an effort to destroy every Creole pig in Haiti. Government officials in Port-au-Prince told the peasants that their pigs would be replaced with pigs purchased in the United States, from Iowa farmers. The promise was kept but the solution was a disaster. The Iowa pigs turned out to be more delicate and more expensive to house and feed than the Creole pigs, and in the end, most didn't survive in their new home.

Père Lafontant—*père* is the French word for "father" or "priest"—was a small but imposing man with a forceful manner, especially when he spoke of life in the central plateau. Like Farmer, the priest believed in liberation theology as a "powerful rebuke to the hiding of poverty," and he worked diligently to bring public awareness to the plight of rural Haitians. He ran a rudimentary one-doctor health clinic in Mirebalais and, along with his wife, helped build schools and organize groups for adult literacy in several small towns, including Cange. The housing in Cange appalled Farmer. Large families lived in small, crude lean-tos with dirt floors and roofs made of banana bark thatch, often patched with rags to stop leaks during the rainy season. Many suffered from one illness or another, Farmer observed, and Lafontant confirmed that there was little or no medicine for them. Everyone looked dejected, as if unsure if they had a future. They seemed like people Farmer had seen in waiting rooms in the dreadful public clinics he'd visited throughout the country. It was as if all of Cange were one of those waiting rooms, he thought.

Farmer didn't stop in Cange for long, not on this first visit, because his goal was to see as much of Haiti as possible. He traveled in tap-taps, on buses, and on foot, sometimes hitching rides, always taking notes and snapping photos. He came down with dysentery and ended up in a grubby hospital in Port-au-Prince, on a floor that lacked a toilet. He refused to go back to the States—at least, that's what he told an American public health expert who visited him in the hospital—but he was thinking, "Please take me home." When he recovered, however, he went on sampling Haiti—attending Voodoo ceremonies, volunteering to assist doctors at Hôpital St. Croix in the town of Leogane, and conversing in Creole with peasant farmers. He didn't trust books in his study of anthropology; he wanted to hear what locals had to say about their lives. Most echoed the feeling of Père Lafontant that the poor had been screwed over by the rich, but that God loved them more than the rich, and their cause to acquire basic human rights was just. They didn't want to wait until the afterlife for things to get better, as some missionaries were resigned to telling them. They wanted justice and equality now. The message suited Farmer temperamentally, because for all his scholarly understanding of developing nations' problems, his strongest impulses were pragmatic. He might seem like a nerd, he once told me, but he saw himself as "an action kind of guy."

An American physician whom Farmer befriended at Hôpital St. Croix gave him another valuable insight. The doctor, who was leaving the country after a year of service, confided that while he loved the Haitian people, he couldn't wait to return to the States. Living without basic amenities such as electricity had worn him down. Farmer asked if he wasn't going to miss the work he'd done, because there was so much disease and the need for medical services was so urgent. In Hôpital St. Croix there was sometimes a shortage of blood, and unless a patient could pay for blood to be sent from another hospital, he went without a transfusion and might well die. If you were poor, you were screwed, Farmer thought again. Yet the doctor wasn't focusing on that. "I'm an American, and I'm going home," he said simply.

"Right. Me too," Farmer answered to the statement of being an American, trying to understand and not judge the man. But he realized that Haiti was now so embedded in his mind and heart that he could never abandon the country so quickly. He also puzzled over the doctor's comment, "I'm an American." Farmer wondered how people classified themselves. When it came to medicine, was a physician supposed to have priorities about where he worked according to his citizenship? Weren't we all human beings first? What Farmer knew for certain was he would become a doctor himself, and the sooner he could return to Haiti, the better.

The central belief of liberation theology—to provide "a preferential option for the poor"—seemed like a worthy life's goal to Farmer. "O for the P," as Farmer would eventually abbreviate the term, was a simple concept. It meant providing medicine in the places that needed it the most, and no place was needier than Haiti. He wrote to Ophelia in England, telling her how disappointed he was with Hôpital St. Croix. Farmer had taken it upon himself to raise funds to buy blood-banking equipment for the hospital, and while checks arrived from parents of his friends from Duke, he couldn't stick around long enough to see if the equipment was ever installed. He did learn that hospital management intended to charge patients for its use. The thought so upset him, he informed Ophelia, that he was determined one day to build his own hospital in Haiti, which would include a blood bank, and no one was going to be refused services based on whether they could pay.

Farmer worked for a time at Père Lafontant's clinic, but he began to focus his attention more on Cange, not far up the road from Mirebalais. It was obvious to any outsider that Cange needed some kind of community health system, but the place was so desolate that it was hard to know where to start. Farmer began with a preliminary health census. He enlisted five Haitians who were his age—he required that each had at least one year of junior high school—to go from hut to hut in Cange and two neighboring villages. They recorded the number of families, recent births and deaths, and the apparent causes of morbidity (disease) and mortality. The first survey was just a beginning, Farmer knew, but it confirmed his worst suspicions. Mortality among infants and young children was horrific, and maternal mortality, the deaths of mothers, often in childbirth, led to a string of catastrophes in surviving family members, from hunger to prostitution.

Farmer's survey was his apprenticeship in public health and medicine as well as anthropology. Determining the effects of Voodoo on everyone's life was especially important. A doctor who didn't understand local culture might mistake patients' complaints for bizarre superstitions, or be utterly baffled by Haitian logic. None of this would be a mystery to a young ethnographer-doctor who was able to sort out superstition from legitimate symptoms of illness.

Voodoo wasn't the enemy, Farmer knew. He had to make it an ally of the diagnostic process—everything medical needed to be viewed in the context of religious beliefs and social practices.

As he returned to the States, Farmer considered his year in Haiti, where he had met a beautiful and fascinating young woman and learned numerous lessons about poverty, culture, and religion, a success. He was now twenty-four, and his philosophy and worldview had been formed for the rest of his life. He entered Harvard Medical School in the fall of 1984. As he wrote to Ophelia, his goal was to translate his worldview into action, starting in Cange.

In medical school, the first two years consisted mainly of lecture courses, but Farmer managed, with the blessing of the faculty, to make frequent visits to Haiti, taking his notes and textbooks with him. He'd return for his exams and get right back on a plane. Classmates nicknamed him Paul Foreigner. This kind of commuting was practically unheard of in medical school, but Farmer maintained excellent grades, some of the best in his class, and it would have been hard for any professor to disapprove of his ambitions. The young man was trying to bring medicine to people without doctors.

CHAPTER 9

WHEN OPHELIA RETURNED to the central plateau to work with Farmer in the summer of 1985, she noticed changes in him. He often wore a wooden cross outside his shirt, and he rarely missed Sunday church services. Years later he told me how religious faith was so disdained at Harvard and so important to the poor—not just in Haiti but elsewhere—that he'd become convinced that faith must be something good. He wanted to believe that someone omniscient—an all-knowing God—was keeping score of what happened on earth, and just maybe it was time for things to change.

At Duke and Harvard, he saw that most students chased

money, power, or a sense of personal advancement, but Farmer's motives for becoming a doctor were different. Helping the poor was part of his worldview, in which spirituality definitely played a part. If one wanted a place to look for God, he had concluded, it should be in the suffering of the poor. Farmer had never cared much about the religious dogma he'd been taught as a child, and he still didn't believe in most of it now. He would say, "I'm looking for something in the sacred texts that says, 'Thou shalt not use condoms.'" Whatever best prevented the spread of infectious diseases—like using condoms when having sex—had to be okay in the eyes of God. Practicality and common sense became pillars of his religious faith.

Being with Ophelia after her two years away also deepened his feelings for her, and hers for him. One morning in Mirebalais, they both skipped church, electing instead to watch the heavy downpour from Père Lafontant's empty rectory. The rain pounded the roof, and there was a fire in the courtyard lit for Sunday dinner. Their emotions for each other were too strong to resist.

She spent that whole summer in Haiti with him. In the evenings, over coffee, she'd help him with his formal medical education, which he'd summarized on thousands of highly imaginative flash cards. One side of a card might read, "Show me, sir, the lesions of Horner's syndrome & oculomotor nerve paralysis. And what the divvil's an Argyll Robertson pupil?" The answers on the back were equally whimsical and often included drawings—many of them lovely, thought Ophelia—in this case a sketch of the neural pathways of the eye.

Farmer rarely missed an answer. His quickness and accuracy at first entertained Ophelia, but she began to wonder why he couldn't miss once in a while, allowing her a chance to correct him. In general, she noticed that Pel didn't like making mistakes or being wrong. His perfectionism seemed absolute, even when they took walks to other villages and he insisted on quizzing her about the Latin names of plants they saw. He'd been doing this since they first met, but increasingly he was making her feel uneducated. When they visited local families, they were often served food that both of them found unsavory, but they would go ahead and eat it. One time she couldn't quite make herself eat what looked like a fried egg afloat in pig fat and gristle, so Farmer slurped it down for her. He was only saving face with the family, she knew, but she felt she had somehow failed in his eyes.

Coming down a steep trail with Paul one day, she momentarily lost her footing. Someone called out in Creole, "Watch your step!" An elderly Haitian came over and offered her his walking stick. Did they think she was a weakling? "No, I'm fine!" she said.

Paul's face looked stern. "Don't refuse something like that," he said to her emphatically. "It's an incredible gift."

Of course he was right, she thought, but her cheeks

burned. Another time, sleeping in different quarters in Cange—the patriarch of the place was, after all, a priest—Ophelia was determined to rise early in the morning, ahead of Paul. She set the alarm clock for five, only to wake to the sound of Farmer's voice, singing up to her from the courtyard below. She lay in bed thinking, "I just want to do something better than him. For a moment."

That summer Farmer expanded and refined the health census he'd begun in 1983. Ophelia worked on gathering data, which meant walking from village to village, sometimes with Farmer, other times with local youths he'd recruited. The heat was oppressive and her fair-skinned face turned bright red from the sun. The peasants would offer her a chair and a cool drink. Her Creole had improved substantially, allowing her to take accurate notes as they described their various pains and miseries. She often noticed a distinctive smell inside the crowded huts. "Not smelly socks stinky," she told me, "but the close smell of people in poverty. Many hungry people breathing."

Sometimes she visited houses where people were dying, and often, especially in Cange, there were children with diarrheal diseases that could be fatal. To get water from the stagnant reservoir, somebody had to climb down a steep eight-hundred-foot hillside, gathering their water in gourds or recycled plastic jugs. Back in the huts, the water would sit uncovered for days, attracting dirt and flies. After Ophelia and Farmer finished their revised census, a

Haitian American engineering team, with funding from the same South Carolina church that had been helping Père Lafontant, devised a plan to pump fresh water from an underground river at the base of the steep hill. The project proved successful, with communal spigots in Cange ultimately making fresh water available to everyone. As soon as this happened, Ophelia told me, diarrheal disease and infant deaths began dropping.

<hr/>

At the Harvard School of Public Health, Farmer had gotten used to hearing that public health problems should be solved with "appropriate technology." That meant one should use the simplest, least expensive technology to complete a job. Père Lafontant despised the concept because he knew what it meant in practical terms: the simplest technology was for the poor, while the rich had the resources to afford the best technology. The Haitian American engineering feat at Cange was not a case of simple technology; the pipe bringing up the clean, sparkling water from the underground river could not have happened without sophisticated engineering. Whatever the price of saving lives, Farmer and Lafontant believed, it must be paid. Every time Farmer looked at a pamphlet from WHO explaining, for example, how to equip a third-world clinic laboratory using one sink instead of two, and solar power instead of electricity, he threw the pamphlet away. The global health care system, and institutions such as WHO that wrote its standards, had the wrong mind-set. Farmer was determined that one day he would help change it.

Before he could influence global policy, however, he knew he'd have to demonstrate his approach to effective public health care in the central plateau. His Cange census allowed him to begin building files and to create a baseline against which future censuses could measure how well his system was working. He planned for what he called a "first line of defenses" in the central plateau communities: vaccination programs, protected water supplies and sanitation, and a small army of trained people from the villages—community health workers—to administer medicines and give health classes. There would be special classes for women to reduce local maternal mortality. If someone was gravely ill with an infectious disease such as TB, malaria, or typhoid, the patient would be sent to the clinic, Bon Sauveur, that he and Père Lafontant were building in Cange. The clinic was the second line of defense. One day, Farmer promised himself, attached to the clinic would be a legitimate hospital, with equipment as good as anything found in a developed nation.

Farmer was quick to give credit to Père Lafontant both for his vision for improving life in Cange and for his ability to raise funds with the help of the South Carolina church. When the priest had built his first school, it had only a thatched roof, and classes that couldn't fit inside were held under a mango tree. In the early 1980s, Lafontant supervised the construction of a much larger, two-story building in Cange, on a small hillside plateau above Highway 3. Children flocked to the facility. To an outsider, building a school before there was a medical clinic, or someone to deal with the problems of hunger and homelessness, was illogical, but Farmer and Lafontant understood that the school meant hope and empowerment. One peasant woman explained, "A lot of us wondered what would have happened if we had known how to write. If we had known how to write, perhaps we wouldn't be in this situation now." To build a school was to unite the practical and the moral, Farmer realized. He would say, "Clean water and health care and school and food and tin roofs and cement floors, all of these things should constitute a set of basics that people must have as birthrights."

Farmer had a grand vision but only limited fundraising experience. Two years earlier, in 1983, just starting medical school, he'd visited a charity in Boston called Project Bread. Père Lafontant had told him how much Cange could use a bakery. Farmer asked the Project Bread director for a few thousand dollars. He was told he was in luck, as the organization had a donor who specifically wanted money to go to feeding the poor in Haiti. When Farmer asked for the name of the donor, he was told the person wanted to be anonymous. A year later Farmer published an essay about his work in Haiti, "The Anthropology Within," in a Harvard Medical School publication, and the anonymous donor suddenly surfaced. He had read Farmer's piece and wanted to meet him. "He sounds like a winner," he reportedly said.

"If he wants to meet me, tell him to come to Haiti," Farmer replied.

The man was Tom White, the owner of Boston's largest commercial construction firm. They met on a hot, windy afternoon at the Port-au-Prince airport. Farmer had imagined a portly, cigar-smoking type who made backroom deals with the Massachusetts Bay Transit Authority. The gentleman who stepped off the plane was in his sixties, with a pink face. He was dressed in golfing clothes and looked slightly ill at ease. In his pocket was a roll of cash that he quickly dispersed to beggars, an act that Farmer didn't find objectionable but which he nonetheless deemed insufficient. Tom White met Farmer's "WL" definition: someone who donated money but didn't understand the depth of third-world problems or how to really fix them. As Farmer drove his visitor on Highway 3 to Cange, he narrated Haiti. White seemed appropriately horrified by Farmer's stories and by the poverty around him, not to mention the condition of the road, yet he didn't talk much. Farmer kept pushing him, wanting to know his politics. Until he had more information, Farmer was cool and distrustful, even a little prickly, White told me, remembering the moment.

"Well, I didn't vote for Reagan," White finally remarked.

"What do you mean?" said Farmer. "So you voted against your own interests?"

"Is that a sin?" said White.

Farmer began to relax and become warmer. He saw that he had a donor he could trust, maybe a WL who could be educated about the real challenges of abating poverty. The next time Farmer returned to Boston, White took him to lunch. One of their conversations was about guilt. White said he thought it was a useless emotion, having felt guilty about his divorce from his first wife and learning nothing from that emotion. All he did was beat himself up, he said. Farmer disagreed. He said that guilt—at least the kind some rich people felt toward the poor—allowed money to flow to the clinics and schools in the central plateau.

White acknowledged Farmer's point—that kind of guilt could make a difference in the world. He had grown up in an Irish Catholic household devastated by his father's drinking, yet earned his way into Harvard, fought hero- ically in World War II, and came home to take over what was left of his father's small construction company. With hard work White built it into a hugely profitable enterprise, but he didn't like spending money on himself. He had been giving away money for years, to Catholic charities and needy friends, even before he had much of his own; now he found himself on boards of prestigious organizations and becoming friends with important politicians and dignitar- ies. Yet he was generally uncomfortable among the rich and famous. He was looking for someone to direct him to using his dollars in a way that would make a *real* difference in the world.

White found it easy to imagine himself a Haitian. A child with big eyes and a memorable smile, encountered in a dirt-floor hut, made him feel like bringing over the company bulldozers. "For Christ's sake," he'd say to Farmer or Père Lafontant, "put a tin roof on and pour a concrete floor. I'll give you the money." Every time he jogged along Highway 3 he couldn't help thinking, "This would be so easy to fix."

When Farmer remained in Haiti, White found himself running errands in Boston for projects in Cange, picking up things like sinks and other supplies that couldn't be found in Haiti. On his dime, White had everything shipped to Cange. He always avoided the media and never asked for any recognition. One time when they were together in Boston, White said, "You know, Paul, sometimes I'd like to chuck it all and work as a missionary with you in Haiti." Farmer thought for a while, then said, "In your particular case, that would be a sin." He needed Tom White in Boston, using his influence where it had the most impact.

A couple of years later, White helped Farmer realize his next step of creating an organization that would support the growing health system around Cange. He gave a million dollars in seed money and hired an attorney to draw up papers for Partners in Health and its corresponding sister organization in Haiti, Zanmi Lasante. PIH would now be able to solicit tax-free contributions from around the world that would be funneled right to Cange, and White would eventually realize his goal of giving away all of his personal fortune in his lifetime.

CHAPTER 10

OPHELIA ATTENDED SCHOOL in England for most of
the year, but she returned to Cange every summer from
1985 until 1989. They were months of nearly constant work.
Keeping up with Paul as he worked in the clinic required
patience and stamina on her part. Ophelia helped with virtually anything he requested of her, from research to dealing with patients, but she was human, too. When she asked
P.J. to have a late lunch with her in the simple house he
lived in, up the hill across from the clinic, she felt that he
did so reluctantly. She could imagine what he was thinking: "There are so many patients to see and treat, and I need
to spend every minute with them."

From time to time she longed to get away from Cange and its desolation. She'd talk P.J. into weekend trips to Port-au-Prince, ostensibly to buy medicine and equipment for the clinic. But Cange was always on Farmer's mind. Once Ophelia asked if they could stop to buy some Diet Coke on the way.

He said, "We don't have time. We can't do it."

His words nettled her. She understood that he wanted to get back to Cange and that making the stop would mean not just a twenty-minute detour, but also walking past the beggars into a supermarket that served the Haitian elite. He seemed to be saying that if he and the peasantry could get along without things like Diet Coke, so could she. In a way he was right, she knew—he was right about so many things—but she started in on him, accusing him of self-righteousness. Their arguing reached such a pitch that he stopped the truck and ordered her out. She didn't obey, feeling both offended and exultant, smiling inwardly, thinking, "*Yes!* I got to you. You have this human quality. You're flawed."

One particular trip to Port-au-Prince stood out in her memory. It was 1986, not long after Baby Doc Duvalier had been forced from power by a popular uprising. A military junta had filled the vacuum of power, and the corruption and cruelty were as bad as ever. As Farmer and she were leaving the capital, Ophelia suddenly smelled burning tires. When Haitians wanted to protest or tried to block a street, they often set tires on fire. A minute later Ophelia saw what in Haiti is called *kouri*—a stampede of people in the street—running for their lives, pursued by army trucks mounted with guns. Gunfire erupted. Their car was suddenly surrounded by demonstrators, some of them wounded. Farmer let several into the back of his car.

"P.J., let's get out of here!" Ophelia said.

They drove to Père Lafontant's house and Farmer let Ophelia out. "I have to go back, Min," he said.

"P.J., please don't."

There was nothing she could do to stop him. Farmer returned to the demonstrations and found more bloodied civilians. He put as many into his car as possible and drove them to a hospital. He came out of the day unscathed, but from that moment on Ophelia worried often about P.J.'s safety. Yet there was no telling Paul what he should or shouldn't do. "It was very important for Paul to witness things," Ophelia would say, looking back. She went on, "That smell of burning tires never quite leaves you. The smell is forever associated for me with political violence." For many years to come, the smell of revolt, of roadblocks and massacres, would be an abiding odor in Haiti and in Ophelia's life and Paul's.

* ◄ • ► *

In 1988 Ophelia came to Boston to live with Paul. He was entering a new phase of medical school known as clinical rotations—month-long stretches of training at Boston hospitals—but whenever possible he shuttled between Boston and Cange. His new priority, now that Tom White had established Partners in Health as a legal fund-raising entity, was to find money for expanding his clinic. Ophelia had raised some funds when she'd been back in England, and now began working in the PIH office in Boston, a shabby one-room office above a seafood restaurant. Farmer convinced a well-heeled Duke classmate, Todd McCormack, to join the PIH board of advisers, as did, some months later, a fellow Harvard anthropology and medical student named Jim Yong Kim. Farmer wanted to surround himself with people, particularly friends, who shared the same zeal and commitment to fighting poverty on a global scale, but starting with Haiti. PIH believed in sending resources directly to Cange, down "the steep gradient of inequality." Farmer called it a show of "pragmatic solidarity." Helping the most desperate people first was how they would change the way the world perceived poverty.

Jim Kim, a Korean American, shared the same principles as Farmer, but he had a different view about how to achieve them. He believed that PIH couldn't isolate itself. If it wanted to make an impact on global poverty, it would have to deal with organizations such as UNESCO and WHO and try to influence their policy making. Jim, Ophelia, and Paul would go out to dinner and talk about these matters until the restaurant closed. Then they'd retreat to Jim's apartment and talk some more. Often they stayed in one of Tom White's houses. Tom would go to bed long before everyone else and in the morning growl at them, "I don't know what you guys talk about all night long."

One of the PIH board's first decisions was to build another school in a village near Cange. Ophelia's father put up the money—about $4,500—and because PIH had no red tape and little overhead, the school was built right away. Farmer called this decision an AMC—"area of moral clarity." It was like when Père Lafontant installed communal latrines in Cange, which all but eradicated typhoid in the village. The world as a whole might not be black-and-white, Jim, Ophelia, and Paul thought, but there were some situations where it was perfectly clear what needed to be done. AMCs abounded in Haiti.

One evening, hurrying around before catching his flight to Haiti, Farmer stepped off a curb and was struck by a car. His knee was shattered. He languished for three weeks at Massachusetts General Hospital, then returned with a huge cast on his leg to the apartment he shared with Ophelia. Farmer was more anxious than ever, frustrated that he couldn't return to Cange. In the next month Ophelia did her best to nurse him, but even before the accident, she said, she was feeling "the strain of living with a fellow who was in love with something else, something I couldn't compete with, even if I wanted to." When he was able to fly again, he'd sometimes catch a flight to Haiti just for the weekend, returning to Boston only to meet medical school obligations, leaving almost no time to be with Opelia.

"Please don't go," she said to him once. "Stay with me."

"Come with *me*," he replied.

They argued. "I was clear about what I wanted to do with my life, and I thought you wanted to join me," Paul said.

Ophelia knew that was true. It was almost impossible to argue with him on any logical basis. Emotionally, she was feeling starved. They patched up their quarrel, but inwardly she knew something had ended. When he proposed marriage a couple of years later, she found it hard to say no but impossible to say yes.

Lovely Pel,

My inability to promise a life with you, as your wife, does not stem from a lack of love or deep, deep commitment to you. Indeed, as you probably know, I have not felt a serious ounce for anyone but you since 1983. My decision was based, instead, on trying to envision our life together and I saw us not matching (the only way we didn't fit). For a long time I thought I could live and work in Haiti, carving out a life with you, but now I understand that I can't. And that's simply not compatible with your life—the life you once told me you would like to lead even ten years ago . . . namely your unswerving commitment to the poor, your limitless schedule and your massive compassion for others. . . .

Hurt by Ophelia's rejection, Paul said, "If I can't be your husband, I can't be your friend. It would be too painful."

For a time after that, she got her only news of him through Jim Kim. Away from Farmer, her interest in becoming a medical doctor waned. Still, the life she and Paul had shared was not something she was willing to throw away. She intended to remain a part of PIH and of Paul's life. Eventually, she would take over the management of PIH's finances and start an endowment.

Ultimately, Paul and Ophelia adjusted to a new relationship. Fresh off the plane from Haiti, after a week or a month away, many times she was the first one he'd call or visit. "Min!" he'd cry, wearing a wild-looking grin, blushing, and reach out his arms to her. He seemed to feel that he could tell her anything, now that he had no formal obligations to her. Being his confidante, she felt essential to him, in some ways closer to him than ever. She'd say to herself sometimes, "Being his wife would have been no bargain. But to be his friend is simply wonderful."

CHAPTER 11

———— ⋅•≻⋅ ⋅≺•⋅ ————

WHEN FARMER RETURNED to Cange, confined mostly to a wheelchair, his shattered knee still healing in a cast, he had more to worry about than his health. In addition to launching a study to improve TB treatment in the central plateau, he was faced with an exploding AIDS epidemic. As his leg mended and he became ambulatory, he also confronted growing political violence when he traveled to Port-au-Prince. Several times he was in churches when shooting started, and he often took refuge behind a pillar. He verified that Haitian army soldiers were shooting unarmed demonstrators, entering urban hospitals and threatening staff, sometimes executing patients. The army's paramilitaries had massacred scores of voters at polling places.

Haitians had been hopeful after Baby Doc Duvalier and his secret police had been chased from power, yet the military leaders of the new junta were even more brutal. Protests in the capital and in smaller cities happened almost every day. The man who was inspiring the protests was a priest named Jean-Bertrand Aristide. His sermons were given in a small Catholic church—St. Jean Bosco in Port-au-Prince—which had become the progressive, liberation theology church in Haiti. After one Sunday Mass, Farmer joined a small group that went to see Aristide. The fearless priest had already survived several assassination attempts, including the firebombing of his church, which had been arranged by the mayor of Port-au-Prince. Farmer found Aristide's life inspirational. The priest cared more about making lasting changes in his country than about his own life. The men already knew each other from Farmer's work in the central plateau, and their friendship only strengthened after they met again at St. Jean Bosco. Farmer was hoping Aristide would openly challenge the junta by running for president. Someone, he knew, had to end the turmoil and bloodshed and their inevitable by-product, the worsening of Haiti's already horrendous public health. Farmer was betting on the priest.

Back in Cange, Farmer continued to work on his anthropology PhD. His thesis was called "AIDS and

Accusation," and part of it centered on "the geography of blame." Haiti had been scapegoated by sociologists and even doctors as the origin of the AIDS virus, or if not the origin, the place to which it had spread from Africa on its way to the United States, Farmer wrote. The Centers for Disease Control, a federal U.S. agency, had gone so far as to identify Haitians as a "risk group," along with several other groups whose names happened to begin with an *h*—homosexuals, hemophiliacs, and heroin users. The publicity had done enormous damage to the fragile Haitian economy, Farmer added, and further stereotyped Haiti as a place so wretched and cursed that the outside world would consider it hopeless, a place to avoid under any circumstances. Yet Farmer only had to look at the changes in Cange from when he'd first visited the settlement six years earlier. It had grown from 107 to 178 households. Thanks to Père Lafontant and his wife, and Tom White's financial support, tin roofs were now common; groves of trees had been planted; there was also an artisans' workshop and a bigger school; and the Bon Sauveur clinic had expanded its services. And there were the communal water fountains, connected to the sparkling clean underground river. Cange no longer looked like a miserable encampment of refugees, Farmer thought dryly, just a typical, extremely poor Haitian village. He still had miles to go.

In the spring of the following year, 1990, Harvard bestowed on Farmer both his PhD in anthropology and his MD. His thesis, "AIDS and Accusation," won a prize and was published as a book by a university press. The Brigham accepted Farmer and Jim Kim into its prestigious residency program in internal medicine. At thirty-one years old, Farmer had dealt with more varieties of illness than most physicians would see in a lifetime. He made no secret that he would continue his unorthodox habit of flying to Haiti as often as possible, spending half his time in Cange and half at the Brigham to meet his residency requirements. For this he had the support of several important faculty members who had taken a liking to Farmer and admired his accomplishments. For the next four years they would continue to defend him from the rivalries and rules of academia. Lives of service depend on the lives of support, Farmer would come to say. He'd gotten help from so many, starting at Harvard.

By late 1990, it seemed possible that Haiti might have a legitimate national election, though it wouldn't happen without resistance from the junta. Military checkpoints were suddenly everywhere on Highway 3, and Farmer, like everyone else, was expected to pay a bribe. Sometimes the soldiers confiscated medical equipment he was bringing to the clinic. In the Port-au-Prince office of Zanmi Lasante, he received death threats on the phone, possibly because of his friendship with Jean-Bertrand Aristide. Farmer refused to be intimidated. When the priest finally declared his candidacy for president, Farmer wrote in a journal, "Perhaps this is a singular chance to change Haiti."

Despite the jeopardy he knew he was placing himself in,

he became a vocal supporter of Aristide. When the elections were finally held, and certified by outside observers that included former President Jimmy Carter, Farmer was in Port-au-Prince. Aristide walked away with 67 percent of the vote and wasted no time promising to deal with the vast inequalities of his country. Farmer knew that liberation theology would be part of the platform of change. Feeling exultant as he drove back to Cange, he considered the real victors of the election to be the Haitian peasantry, like his friends and patients at the clinic. They'd braved intimidation, even massacres, to vote. After centuries of misery, slavery, injustice, and foreign interference, the people of Haiti had claimed their country.

Farmer had many reasons to be optimistic when he returned to Boston and the Brigham in the summer of 1991. Aristide's government had assumed power. There were no more checkpoints when Farmer drove to and from Port-au-Prince. The Haitian Ministry of Health had begun working with Zanmi Lasante on AIDS prevention in the central plateau. And PIH had raised most of the money to begin construction on a hospital in Cange.

At the end of September, Farmer planned a quick trip to Haiti to check on things. When he reached Miami for his connecting flight to Port-au-Prince, however, the sign above the check-in desk read CANCELED. No one at the airport could offer him an explanation. Concerned, he turned on the television news in his motel room. The Haitian army had overthrown Aristide's new government after only a few months in power. The next day, Farmer was stunned again when he learned that the junta had put his name on a list of personae non gratae—"unwelcome people." Fearing arrest if he flew to Haiti, he returned to Boston, bitter and disappointed. In the next few months he made repeated phone calls to Père Lafontant and his wife in Haiti, asking when it would be safe for him to come. The priest ultimately bribed a Haitian army colonel to remove Farmer's name from the list.

He was quickly on a plane to Port-au-Prince, though not without a case of nerves when he walked through immigration and showed his passport. No one detained him, but on the ride to Cange he was disheartened to see military checkpoints and roadblocks in place once more. Two days later, working at the clinic, beginning to feel calmer, he was approached by a former TB patient, a young woman with a baby. In a frantic voice she told him how local authorities had beaten her husband and he was dying. Farmer quickly packed his doctor's bag and hiked with her across the Péligre Dam to a hut on the other side of the reservoir.

He found the woman's husband lying on the dirt floor, beaten to unconsciousness. Farmer did all he could with the equipment in his bag, but he knew even the Brigham's emergency room probably would have failed. Afterward, Farmer recorded the wounds:

On January 26, Chouchou, a handsome man in his mid-twenties, was scarcely recognizable. His face, and especially his left temple, was misshapen, swollen, and lacerated; his ... mouth was a coagulated pool of dark blood; he coughed up more than a liter of blood in his agonal moments. Lower down, his neck was peculiarly swollen, his throat collared in bruises, the traces of a gun butt. His chest and sides were badly bruised, and he had several fractured ribs. . . . Chouchou's back and thighs were striped with deep lash marks. His buttocks were hideously macerated, his skin flayed down to the exposed gluteal muscles. Many of these stigmata appear to be infected.

The people who did this probably weren't far away. Farmer didn't dare go back by the same route, on foot over the dam. He borrowed a canoe from a local fisherman and paddled it back across the reservoir.

Incensed by the brutality, he reported the atrocity to Amnesty International, an organization that documents cases of human rights abuse. He also wrote a piece called "A Death in Haiti," which the *Boston Globe* published under someone else's name. Chouchou's grave offense had been to mutter a disparaging comment about the condition of Highway 3, overheard by a soldier not even in uniform. Farmer remembered all of his patients—he kept track of their faces and quirks and the dates he had seen them, using mnemonic devices, just like his flash cards in medical school. The problem, of course, was that he remembered some patients all too well. In later years he didn't like to talk about Chouchou. He told me, "I take active precautions not to think about him." By then he'd already described the case in print several times. To me, he simply said, "He died in the dirt."

CHAPTER 12

A꙰s the junta continued to rule with an iron fist, Farmer became increasingly frustrated and angry. With Aristide out of power, there was little hope for peace, let alone real change. The central plateau was known for its pro-Aristide leanings, and the junta kept a close eye on places like Zanmi Lasante and troublemakers like Farmer and Père Lafontant. A defiant Farmer wasn't even polite to the soldiers who stopped him at the checkpoints, and when they came to snoop around the clinic, he didn't bother to hide his books about Che Guvera or Castro, or an iron sculpture that was a symbol of Aristide's movement and hung in his office. Ophelia visited him occasionally in the early 1990s, but with so many soldiers around, she quickly became concerned for her life as well as Paul's. The army could swoop in one night and massacre everyone, doctors and patients, she thought. The staff promised to defend Zanmi Lasante, but no one had weapons. She knew Paul was aware of the possibility of complete disaster, but she also knew he wasn't about to shut down the clinic.

On one trip back to Boston, he asked Tom White to give him ten thousand dollars in cash, which he planned to smuggle into Haiti and turn over to the underground pacifist resistance. When Jim Kim found out, he was alarmed and said to Farmer, "You're no use to anyone as a martyr." Jim was used to his friend raising his voice when he wanted to make a point, but this time Farmer screamed at him, *"What do you want me to do?"* Jim went silent. Farmer smuggled the money into Haiti.

With his frustration boiling over into recklessness, Farmer took more and more chances. He invited a group of influential nuns from the Catholic group Pax Christi to Haiti, hoping when they returned to the States they would spread the truth about the junta's abuses. Twice at roadblocks, soldiers searched both him and the nuns. One soldier ordered Farmer to say "Long live the Haitian army."

"I'm not going to say that," he answered.

"You better say that." The soldiers raised their weapons.

"Okay," he said sweetly.

One day a soldier entered the clinic compound carrying

a gun. Farmer came out to the courtyard, weaving through the usual large crowd. "You can't bring a gun in here," he said, confronting the soldier.

"Who are you to tell me what I can do?"

Farmer thought for a moment. "I'm the person who's going to take care of you when you get sick," he answered.

It was a pivotal moment. The soldier couldn't back down in front of the crowd, and Farmer had subtly declared he wasn't backing down, either. As the tension rose, he considered that maybe this time he'd gone too far, putting hundreds of people at risk. Everyone waited out the silence. Finally the soldier growled some menacing words, then turned and disappeared. Farmer's answer must have struck a chord with the man, because in fact Farmer was the best doctor in the central plateau, and Zanmi Lasante was the only place where anyone, soldiers or civilians, could receive decent medical care, no questions asked. The relief Farmer felt after the showdown was followed by reprimands from his staff. He understood he could not put himself, and others, in jeopardy again. Shots had been fired at the Zanmi Lasante office in Port-au-Prince, and Père Lafontant had closed it down. From that moment on, Farmer curtailed his travel within the country. He would only go to the capital to catch a flight out.

He returned to Boston in the summer of 1993 to receive his MacArthur "genius" grant, which brightened his mood because he had a good use for the $220,000 tax-free award—

it would go straight to PIH. When he returned to Haiti, however, the political tensions and violence had worsened, and his mood turned somber again. The body count kept growing. Three close friends of Farmer's had been murdered. Borrowing money from Ophelia, he flew to Quebec City—one of his favorite places to retreat—and, shutting himself in a hotel room for ten days, wrote 220 pages of a draft of a book that would ultimately be titled *The Uses of Haiti*. It is the most passionate of Farmer's books, exploring the complicated history of American policy toward Haiti. Trying to unravel the evil of the dark, brooding centuries of slavery and oppression, the book identifies too many villains and not enough heroes. The United States had intervened so many times without making lasting, positive changes.

Now there was talk that the new Clinton administration might send troops once again into Haiti, to put Aristide back in power. Farmer was reluctant to raise his hopes too high. In early 1994, just before *The Uses of Haiti* was published, he wrote in an editorial for the *Miami Herald*, "Should the U.S. military intervene in Haiti? We already have. Now we should do so in a new way, to restore democracy." The editorial was mentioned on the government radio station in Haiti, and the junta promptly declared that Farmer had slandered the Haitian government. Once more he was put on its official personae non gratae list. He moped around the Boston PIH office for a while, then went on a lecture tour, hitting small towns in Maine, Texas, Kansas, and Iowa, explaining the situation in Haiti to anyone who would listen. He even testified before a congressional committee, and later got into a shouting match with an American general who claimed Farmer was "totally out in left field." During a radio interview in Fort Lauderdale, one caller told him, referring to the boats of Haitian refugees fleeing the violence and poverty, "We can't have Haitians coming into our country."

"Why not?" Farmer said. "*My* family are boat people."

The host, understandably, didn't get it. "Dr. Farmer, are you Haitian?"

Farmer ultimately thought, "Screw this. I want to go back to my clinic." He returned to Haiti in mid-October 1994, the day Aristide was reinstated as president, about three years after he had been deposed.

⬥⬥⬥⬥

It would be a few months before Farmer encountered Jon Carroll, the army captain, in the central plateau, and I got my first glimpse of the American doctor and his thoughts. It was the beginning of my learning curve on Haiti. Three years of military rule had resembled a war and caused a public health disaster. The United Nations estimated that about eight thousand people were killed, most of them murdered by the Haitian army and its paramilitaries. Many others—maybe thousands—drowned while fleeing the country in small, crude boats. There were no statistics about how many others died from infectious and other diseases. Farmer could only make guesses, based on the wreckage he returned to at Cange.

In spite of the junta's rule, Père Lafontant had managed to get the new hospital built, thanks to the funding from PIH and Tom White. All of the other Zanmi Lasante projects in the villages around Cange had been interrupted—its programs for women's literacy, for vaccinating children, for sanitation and clean water, for distributing condoms and other AIDS-prevention measures. During the three-year reign of terror, Zanmi Lasante was the only place that dared to treat people who had been beaten or shot. Afraid of reprisals from the military if they did seek help, many Haitians stayed away unless their health problems became critical. Under military rule, the number of people with chronic malnutrition, tuberculosis, and measles jumped dramatically. Particularly striking were new cases of AIDS—a 60-percent rise in three years.

Another casualty of the brutal regime was the Zanmi Lasante staff. Not that they were hunted or killed, but many left the clinic from fear, and Farmer noted the "paralysis" and "lassitude" among those who stayed behind. Haitian doctors, who were used to seeing death, became even more hardened or indifferent to the suffering around them. Even the most optimistic staff began to cancel meetings, abandon research projects, and shelve any new ideas. Life was all about survival.

But the situation was far from hopeless, Farmer

thought, glad to be back. He intended to keep expanding Zanmi Lasante. He was thirty-five now, on the rise in both medicine and anthropology, and the author of two published books and about two dozen articles. Partners in Health had changed offices as it began to grow to about a dozen staff—about half volunteers, the rest underpaid employees. They managed an AIDS-prevention program in Boston and provided medical and social services to the poor. With small sums and advice, they also supported projects in far-flung places such as Chiapas, Mexico.

In PIH's 1993 annual report, Farmer wrote that the organization should never change its basic mission—serving Haiti—or soften its message in order to broaden its appeal. In his mind, discipline and focus were paramount; energy was not to be squandered. But, in fact, a big change in PIH was coming. They were about to become players in international health.

Part III
MÉDICOS
AVENTUREROS

CHAPTER 13

AT THE END of the twentieth century, tuberculosis was killing about two million people a year, more adults than any other infectious disease except for AIDS. TB and AIDS shared what Farmer called "a noxious synergy"—an active case of one often made a latent case of the other active, too. These two plagues, along with other infectious diseases, helped define what Farmer called the "great epi divide" (*epi* being short for *epidemiological,* referring to the study of how diseases spread). Anyone who worked at PIH knew that a simple "epi" map—based on what makes people sick and what kills them, and in what numbers and at what ages—could be coded in two colors. One color would stand for populations, such as those in Europe and North America, who tend to die in their seventies from the illnesses that typically accompany advanced aging; the other color would represent places like Haiti where, on average, people die ten and even forty years earlier, often from violence, hunger, and infectious diseases.

Farmer knew that meager incomes didn't guarantee disease and early death, but the two usually went together. He also knew that many people living on the wrong side of the "great epi divide" had brown or black skin and were female. What they all had in common was poverty. Those who stood the best chance of contracting TB, which was usually spread by the infected person coughing or sneezing, lived in crowded peasant huts, urban slums, shantytowns, prisons, or homeless shelters. Farmer liked to say that tuberculosis made its own preferential option for the poor.

The scale of the problem was vast. According to reliable estimates, about two billion people, almost a third of the world's population, have TB bacilli (bacteria) in their bodies. These germs remain latent in 90 percent of those affected. However, if the bacilli become active—when someone's immune system is compromised, as with AIDS—they multiply rapidly into a bone-eating, lung-consuming illness that, unless treated, is fatal.

First-line antibiotics exist to combat TB, but they aren't readily available in poor countries. Even if a hospital or government agency can afford the antibiotics, the illness is difficult to manage. A person with active TB harbors hundreds of millions of bacilli in his lungs, enough to ensure that a small number will be mutant germs that aren't stopped by anti-TB drugs. In a patient who gets only one antibiotic or inadequate doses of several, or who doesn't take his medicine as instructed, the drug-susceptible bacilli may die off but the drug-resistant mutants will flourish. Doctors have a special name for the illness caused by mutant TB germs: MDR, or multi-drug-resistant tuberculosis.

Farmer knew that MDR was always worse in the places with the fewest resources to deal with it. Because TB was largely concentrated in poor countries, the industrial nations and pharmaceutical companies had all but abandoned the search for new technologies to fight MDR. What drugs did exist were very expensive and often scarce. The treatment could take up to two years—much longer than the treatment for regular TB—and the side effects were often painful for patients. By the mid-1990s, Farmer, to his alarm, had discovered several cases of MDR in Cange. It was the time of the junta, and because he couldn't obtain the necessary medicines, he watched helplessly as the first patient died from the disease. Fearing the possibility of an MDR outbreak, he began assembling the resources at Zanmi Lasante to diagnose and treat it. The expense was born largely by PIH, but soon most MDR cases in Cange were being handled successfully.

In 1995, however, Farmer was shocked by unexpected news. MDR had claimed the life of a close friend, a priest named Jack Roussin, who had been living and working in a shantytown on the outskirts of Lima, the capital of Peru. Farmer had first met Father Jack when the priest was at St. Mary's parish in Roxbury, one of Boston's run-down, largely African American neighborhoods. He was a beefy man with a ruddy complexion and boundless energy. Father Jack had provided Farmer and other financially strapped students with small rooms in the rectory. He was a priest who insisted on getting involved in the real world. He mediated arguments among neighborhood gangs, led vigils against drug dealing, and gave rousing sermons every Sunday. With a sense of humor, he also told off-color stories to the students he befriended. Everyone loved Father Jack, but Farmer also came to respect his intellect and ideals. When Partners in Health was created, he put the priest on its board of advisers.

In the early nineties, Father Jack left St. Mary's to serve the needs of a church in a shantytown called Carabayllo, outside of Lima. His work brought him into contact with people whose health problems were far greater than in Roxbury. Whenever he returned to Boston, he strongly urged Farmer, Ophelia, and Jim to consider starting a PIH project in Lima's slums. The biggest advocate for this bold undertaking, besides Father Jack, was Jim Kim. Farmer remained cautious about overcommitting PIH's limited resources.

In photos from around this time, Jim appears as a neatly groomed, well-proportioned young man, a few inches shorter than Farmer, with jet-black hair swept into a knife-like wave and wire-rimmed glasses over narrow eyes. Like Farmer, he had an expressive face that revealed his enthusiasm and determination, and as second in command at PIH, his role was to keep the wheels of that machine well oiled. Farmer was away much of the time, and even when he was around, darting from meeting to meeting, it was Jim who often made sure he kept to a schedule. Once, as they left the Brigham together, Jim quipped, "Okay, Pel, we're in a hurry. Only one kiss and two hugs per janitor."

Jim had great respect for Farmer, but ultimately he wanted to do more than run the Boston office. He wanted to do in Peru what Farmer had done in Haiti. Father Jack's idea presented the perfect opportunity. With initial funds from Tom White, and Farmer's eventual strong support, Jim created a system of community health workers in Carabayllo. He called the new team Socios en Salud—a Spanish version of Partners in Health.

Flying down to Carabayllo, he worked closely with Father Jack, calling Farmer in Boston or Haiti to keep him informed of their progress. One of Socios en Salud's first projects was to build a pharmacy next to Father Jack's church, to dispense free medicine to the most impoverished people in the slum. Like Farmer in Haiti, Jim had to deal with political uncertainty and violence. Peru was in the midst of a civil war between the government and the

Shining Path guerilla movement, and on midnight one New Year's Eve, while Father Jack was saying Mass, the pharmacy was blown up. Fortunately, no one in the church was hurt. The guerillas claimed they had planted the bomb because the pharmacy represented only "crumbs for the poor"—a mere token of assistance when in fact more substantial changes were needed. Jim simply had the pharmacy rebuilt, though away from the church this time.

Jim was concerned that one of Carabayllo's major health problems might be TB, but Peruvian doctors insisted that the illness was well under control. Years earlier, with advice and assistance from the World Health Organization, a branch of the United Nations, Peru had embarked on a nationwide program of TB diagnosis and treatment. WHO, whose influence and reputation carried a lot of weight in poor countries, had gone so far as declaring Peru's TB program the best in the developing world. The boast seemed justified to Jim and Farmer when they read the official data, which revealed a remarkably low incidence of TB. Even when Farmer began traveling to Lima to conduct a health census for Carabayllo, as he and Ophelia had done in Cange a decade earlier, TB didn't strike him as a problem that couldn't be handled.

Then, in the spring of 1995, Father Jack got sick. After the priest flew to Boston, Jim drove him to the Brigham, where doctors diagnosed tuberculosis. He was put on a standard regimen of four first-line antibiotics, similar to what WHO recommended for anyone who contracted TB.

Only a month after starting the therapy, Father Jack died. A culture showed that the bacilli from his body were resistant to all four of the drugs he'd been given, and to one other first-line antibiotic as well. MDR had taken his life.

On the plane to Lima for Father Jack's memorial service, Farmer wondered to Ophelia what he could have done to save his good friend. It seemed as if he would never stop weeping or blaming himself. Remorse aside, Farmer and Jim knew the clinical facts of Jack's death were the real issue. Most likely Father Jack had contracted MDR from someone in the slums. Yet Farmer, when conducting his health census, had been told that TB was not a special problem in Carabayllo. Even the project director of Socios en Salud—a small, studious Peruvian doctor named Jaime Bayona, handpicked by Jim Kim to run daily operations—told him so. Bayona based his assertion on interviews with doctors and nurses working in government clinics. But Bayona, who both listened and spoke with great care, wasn't totally convinced by what he heard. Clinic staff often lacked conviction in their voices, he told Farmer. He sensed they were hiding something. So the director started asking about MDR in a different way.

"Did you have any TB patients who came and were treated but weren't cured?" Bayona said to a nurse on a visit to one clinic.

"Oh, sure," she replied, and named a specific female patient.

When he located the woman, and determined that

indeed she had MDR, Bayona alerted Farmer. Paul began to worry that if drug-resistant bacilli were infecting people in the slums, how long would it take before the disease spread across all of Lima? In the aftermath of Father Jack's death, he and Jim urged Bayona to step up his visits to public clinics. Bayona would ask his carefully worded question, and more than once a nurse appeared with a stack of patient folders. As she opened them, one said, "We have something here that might interest you, but I can't show it to you."

Bayona wasn't sure why the government wasn't being more cooperative with Socios en Salud, but he quickly learned to read patient files upside down. Again and again, he read stories of patients who hadn't been cured by standard treatment and even retreatment. In the Socios en Salud office in Carabayllo, a worried Bayona would sit at a computer and type up what he'd read, in emails addressed exclusively to Farmer and Kim.

CHAPTER 14

———◆·—·◆———

I SAW CARABAYLLO for the first time when accompanying Farmer on a trip to Lima. Many who lived here, Farmer
told me, came from small villages in the distant Andean
mountains—handsome people with jet-black hair and high
cheekbones. They came looking for what their tiny villages
didn't offer them: jobs, housing, electricity, food, and
schools for their children. To Farmer, it wasn't unlike the
fate of Haitian peasants who left the central plateau and
migrated to the slums of Port-au-Prince. Not finding what
they had hoped or expected, many returned home, but others stayed and tried to eke out a living.

Carabayllo was a meandering, seemingly endless vista

of poverty. I saw roads choked with dilapidated cars, motorcycle rickshaws, and battered minibuses that served as public transportation. Piles of uncollected garbage, along with abandoned vehicles, dotted the banks. Some of the garbage was on fire, smoldering. On cement-block walls, there were signs for bars, nightclubs, hairdressers, and even doctors' offices, with the prices charged for seeing patients painted on the walls. On the lowland beside the road, there were other stores, garages, vendors' carts, and umbrella-covered kiosks. Thick clusters of small houses made of brick and concrete dotted side streets and the lower hillsides. The light poles and paved roads ascended the hills. The pavement turned to dirt, then roads turned into paths, and dwellings grew increasingly forlorn and miserable. Scattered among them were dirt-floored convenience stores, metal-roofed cook shacks (where residents bought dinners because they couldn't afford stoves or the fuel for stoves), barbershops, even graveyards. The air smelled of urine. There were no sewers up there; the only bathrooms were secluded places among the boulders above the last dwellings.

Farmer informed me that Bayona had located rather quickly ten people in Carabayllo with probable MDR, and Jaime was sure he could have found more. To confirm the diagnosis, samples of each patient's TB had to be regrown in cultures and tested for drug susceptibility. Socios en Salud wasn't granted access to Peru's national lab, so Farmer sent the ten specimens back to Boston and deposited them at the Massachusetts State Lab. The results of the cultures were alarming. Most of the ten had TB that was resistant to all five of the first-line antibiotics, just like Father Jack's.

When Farmer flew back to Lima, Bayona accompanied him to a small government health clinic next to Father Jack's former church. The clinic was a dusty little building with a sign on the wall that read *El Progresso*. The ten patients were waiting inside for the American doctor. Farmer examined each one privately. He couldn't yet speak Spanish, so Bayona acted as his interpreter as Farmer put his stethoscope to each person's chest, asked questions, and studied everyone's X-ray. Farmer was a TB expert. He had been diagnosing and treating the illness since he'd first set foot in Haiti. There, he adhered to the same WHO protocol, called DOTS—directly observed treatment short-course chemotherapy—that TB patients in Carabayllo followed. If a Haitian didn't recover from TB, it was usually because, for one reason or another, he failed to take his antibiotics as instructed. But in Carabayllo, Farmer learned that all ten MDR patients had faithfully followed the DOTS protocol. If the first round of antibiotics didn't cure a patient, a re-treatment with the same drugs, plus one, was prescribed. Some patients had undergone a third treatment. Regardless, all ten patients were very sick—some were carried in to see Farmer on stretchers—with TB that was resistant to four or even five drugs. Farmer knew none would survive if something wasn't done for them quickly.

As a medical anthropologist, he had always liked the detective work that came with identifying the origins of a particular pathogen (a virus, bacteria, or anything that causes a disease). Farmer determined from interviews with the ten patients and checking their medical records that all had followed the DOTS procedure to the letter. They hadn't missed taking any of their medications. Also, the quality of the antibiotics had been certified by experts. Farmer also reasoned these patients couldn't have caught the same highly resistant strain, because each one's TB had a slightly different pattern of resistance.

The dynamics of TB make it nearly impossible for a person's infection to acquire resistance to more than one drug at a time, but repeated therapy can create mutant strains resistant to any number of drugs. Farmer concluded this was what must have happened. The ten had gone to the government clinic with TB that was resistant to one or two drugs, and through treatment and repeated retreatment under the DOTS protocol had ended up with four- and five-drug resistance. In taking the antibiotics, they had only been following doctors' orders, and the doctors had only been following the protocol established by WHO, which set the official health policy not only for the Peruvian government but for developing nations around the world.

To Farmer, the conclusion was as painful as it was obvious. If you contracted TB, DOTS didn't always work. And when it didn't, it only made you sicker. Farmer, Kim, and

Bayona collected a number of official WHO statements and read them with dismay. One stated, "In developing countries, people with multi-drug-resistant tuberculosis usually die, because effective treatment is often impossible in poor countries."

With a fatalistic WHO setting the policy, Peruvian clinics didn't provide expensive MDR medicines. Farmer and Bayona knew that most MDR patients couldn't afford to be treated by a private pulmonologist, or lung specialist, though to help a loved one some families tried selling their possessions to pay the doctor's fees. But if the money ran out and the course of drugs still wasn't finished, there were few options for the patients but to return to their shacks on the barren, dusty hillsides of Carabayllo and wait for death to come.

For Partners in Health, there was a bigger principle involved. A TB epidemic, laced with MDR, had occurred in New York City in the late 1980s, largely targeting prisons, homeless shelters, and public hospitals. American agencies had spent about a billion dollars to stop a full-blown outbreak. In Peru, meanwhile, where every year the government made debt payments to American banks and international lending institutions totaling more than a billion dollars, experts in international TB control had decided that MDR was too expensive to treat. To Farmer and Jim, the implications of this shortsightedness were ominous.

CHAPTER 15

———— ◆ •◆ ————

JAIME BAYONA TURNED up dozens of probable cases of MDR in Carabayllo, all by himself, from reading patients' files upside down, in addition to the ten patients Farmer had visited. Farmer suspected the root cause of this growing problem stemmed from decades back—long before Peru adopted the model WHO program in 1991—when drug-resistant strains were spawned by inadequately financed and unsupervised treatment. For the most part, MDR cases had gone unnoticed or were ignored by the government clinics—a TB death was merely recorded as a TB death. Now the developed world, not to mention overpopulated cities such as Lima, could no longer afford to ignore the dire but real possibility that "superbugs"—mutant strains resistant to every known antibiotic—could spread across borders, from slums to entire cities, from poor countries to wealthy ones.

"We've got to say, 'MDR is a threat to everyone,'" Jim declared. "We can scare the world, and if we do this project right, we can have a global impact."

"Okay," Paul said, "but let's try ten patients first."

Farmer started treating patients in August 1996, transporting Zanmi Lasante's TB program to Carabayllo, and tailoring it to MDR and other local circumstances. They already had a group of young Peruvians trained as community health workers, and several skilled Socios en Salud nurses, with Bayona to direct everyone. In addition, Farmer arranged for a top epidemiologist and two medical students from Harvard to live in Carabayllo and work with Socios en Salud. Back in Haiti, he sent daily emails to Lima and devised drug regimens for every patient, exchanging important information with Bayona's team. For a time, Jim Kim did some doctoring himself, before turning his attention to management, training, and fund-raising.

The Peruvian government's clinics and doctors, who had never warmed to Socios en Salud, began characterizing the organization as a group of interfering outsiders. Local physicians didn't want to hear that their model TB program had a flaw. *Médicos aventureros,* one Peruvian doctor cynically labeled Jim and Farmer. That could loosely be translated as "doctors who don't quite know what they're doing." Neither had a license to practice in Peru, and at one point both Jim and Farmer had been threatened with expulsion from the country. Now they learned that they needed official permission to treat every MDR patient they found. Farmer and Jim reluctantly agreed that all patients had to complete the standard WHO protocol before their cases could be deemed "treatment failures." Only then could Socios en Salud take over.

A furious Farmer watched helplessly as one MDR patient died because the Peruvians wouldn't allow Socios en Salud to treat him. Bayona didn't agree with his country's TB policy, but he understood its reasoning. In 1991 Peru had ended decades of improper TB treatment, saved by WHO and the DOTS program. A scandal about MDR now might threaten the government's credibility and hard-won progress. Also, if it allowed Socios en Salud to set a new standard for dealing with MDR in Carabayllo, it would have to meet that standard throughout the country. The government didn't have the money for that unless they took it from their DOTS program, and that would mean returning to the conditions that had spawned MDR in the first place.

In January 1997, Bayona advised Farmer that if they wanted to get around the political roadblocks in Peru, they had to go to higher authorities. Farmer thought he knew a suitable forum. He'd been invited to speak in Chicago the next month to the International Union Against Tuberculosis and Lung Disease, a conservative and influential group of TB experts. Farmer anticipated an uphill battle. Most of the "TB tribe" who knew about Farmer considered Socios en Salud's work unorthodox and Farmer something of a maverick—a clinician too interested in individual patients to comprehend the global TB picture. Farmer didn't want to rile up the establishment, but he was determined to get his points across. He called his speech "Myths and Mystifications About MDR-TB."

As he began talking, he read his audience a quotation from WHO: "MDR is too expensive to treat in poor countries; it detracts attention and resources from treating drug-susceptible disease." This was a myth, Farmer announced to everyone, adding, "Even if TB control is to be governed by considerations of cost-effectiveness, it should be easy to show that failure to diagnose and treat MDR-TB is what is really expensive." He gave an example of a Texas family where one member had exposed nine others to MDR. "Care for these ten persons alone exceeded one million dollars," he reported.

Farmer went on to myth number two: some experts thought that DOTS alone would stop outbreaks of MDR. "Nonsense," he replied. What would happen, he asked, if programs treated drug-susceptible TB successfully and let MDR flourish? This was exactly what was happening in Carabayllo. Currently, he admitted, MDR represented a tiny fraction of all TB cases, but its importance would grow because DOTS would ultimately only amplify already existing drug resistance. He gave examples to support this thesis. In short, he warned, failure loomed for programs that were now judged a success.

Myth number three: MDR was less virulent and contagious than regular TB. Mere wishful thinking, Farmer declared, basically telling his audience they didn't know as much about MDR as he and PIH did. He rejected the idea that he didn't understand the big TB picture. Paying great attention to each patient was not only a moral imperative, he said, it was the only way to understand and control all types of TB in communities, as he'd proven in Cange and was trying to demonstrate in Carabayllo, if the Peruvian government would stop hindering his team's efforts.

He continued his speech, citing more myths about TB, and when he was done the moderator thanked him for giving a provocative talk.

"Excuse me," Farmer replied, "but why do you qualify my talk as provocative? I just said we should treat sick people, if we have the technology."

In Lima a few days later, Jaime Bayona heard a rumor that someone in the audience had called the director of Peru's TB program and told him, "Paul Farmer says you're killing patients." At least Farmer knew that his protest was lodged and the higher authorities had noticed.

CHAPTER 16

IN 1996 FARMER'S personal life changed dramatically: he got married. For two years, with Ophelia encouraging him, he had been courting the Cange schoolmaster's daughter, Didi Bertrand—"the most beautiful woman in Cange," said many at Zanmi Lasante. Most of Cange, four thousand strong, attended the wedding. The couple had a second ceremony in Boston for those who couldn't come to Haiti. Farmer had picked two best men for the ceremonies, and Jim Kim was one of them.

All of this occurred during the hectic early phases of the TB project in Peru. Soon the number of patients being treated by Socios en Salud jumped to about fifty—students, housewives, street vendors, health workers, unemployed youth. Hectic turned into frantic. Fifty cases represented about 10 percent of all active TB cases in the slum, about ten times more than might have been expected. The drugs to treat just one MDR patient cost between $15,000 and $20,000. Jim and Farmer were determined to keep funding the effort, even if that meant convincing the Brigham pharmacy to "loan" them the expensive second-line antibiotics whenever they came to Boston. Ultimately their tab reached $95,000, which Tom White eventually covered with a check to the Brigham.

Now in his seventies, White was prepared to spend his last nickel before he died, yet he began to worry that the cost of Socios en Salud was growing so rapidly that he might run out of funds. Still, he never turned down a request from Farmer, whose early caution about overcommitting PIH resources had given way to around-the-clock urgency. He had been pushing himself hard to meet work demands in Boston, Haiti, and Peru, teaching at Harvard, seeing patients at the Brigham, and, increasingly, making public speaking appearances to raise awareness of the MDR problem as well as raising money.

Farmer had not been feeling well when he gave his Chicago speech in 1997, and the next month, spending time with patients at the Brigham, not only was he easily exhausted, his symptoms included nausea, vomiting, and night sweats. "Oh my God," he suddenly thought. "I've got

MDR." Then he realized, "If I do have MDR, I've exposed all my patients to it."

Yet an X-ray showed his lungs were clear. He called Didi in Paris, where she was in school, and listened to her strong advice that he see a doctor. "Look, I am a doctor," he said. "Let me finish my month at the Brigham and go to Haiti. Then I'll rest."

Farmer was normally a fast diagnostician, but he found himself stalling on his own case. He finally made the right guess on his last day at the Brigham, when the smell of coffee at breakfast made him nauseous. He had had a similarly strong response to pizza the night before. A classic symptom of hepatitis, he thought: revulsion at foods you love. He'd already noticed that his urine was dark, another sign that something was wrong with his liver. But if he had hepatitis, was it type A, B, or C? He'd been vaccinated against B, and he didn't do drugs, so that ruled out C. Type A was usually caused by drinking contaminated water or eating tainted food. Perhaps he'd eaten something in Lima.

When his lab work came back at the end of that day, showing his liver functions at dangerously low levels, Farmer conceded he could no longer tough it out. "All right," he told a hospital colleague. "I give up."

Hepatitis A is rarely fatal, but Farmer's case was so severe that Jim and other doctors worried he might need a liver transplant. Gradually he got better. When he was released from the hospital two weeks later, Ophelia sent him and Didi to a hotel in southern France, Farmer's first real vacation in years. Nine months later, the couple had their first child, a daughter named Catherine.

Hearing Farmer tell this story, I wondered at his recklessness. He'd been preaching the importance of hepatitis A vaccination around the hospital, and he admitted his embarrassment to me. But only, it seemed, for not getting the shot, not for ignoring his symptoms and putting his health in serious jeopardy. He had never told Ophelia or his mother he was sick, and I wondered if that was because they would try to make him stop working. Some doctors tend to feel they're invulnerable, while other people, doctors included, refuse to set their work aside because to do so is inconvenient. In Farmer's case, I thought it was because he couldn't allow himself to be the one to set it aside. A force stronger than his own will had to intervene, like the car that had crushed his knee and put him in a wheelchair in 1988.

Given the responsibilities for other lives he'd taken on, disregarding symptoms of hepatitis for a month seemed almost a selfish act to me. On the other hand, I'd become inclined to hold Farmer to a higher standard than I did most people, including myself. And, as a rule, to see him in action was to excuse him.

• ◄ • ► •

Slowly, the MDR project in Carabayllo, due to Jim Kim's and Jaime Bayona's dogged determination, was making progress with the fifty patients. Farmer and Jim continued to share results with the Peruvian TB doctors, who began to acknowledge Socios en Salud's successes. No one referred to Farmer as a *médico aventurero* anymore. Cynicism had been replaced with respect. One day I accompanied Farmer on a consulting appointment at the Children's Hospital in downtown Lima. He wore a rumpled black suit and a tie. Though traffic delayed his arrival by an hour, the hospital staff and doctors greeted him without being annoyed. If anything, they treated him as someone special, even a hero.

Inside the hospital, marching purposefully down a concrete-walled corridor of the TB wing, his stethoscope draped over his neck as he prepared to see patients, Farmer suddenly stopped. A family of three stood just ahead of him: a five-year-old boy, his mother, and his father. The slender mother, wearing a skirt and a Mickey Mouse T-shirt, shyly hung back, but the father approached Farmer. The men gave each other a fierce bear hug. The boy, slightly chubby, healthy-looking, also ran toward the American doctor, though with an odd, waddle-like gait. Farmer crouched down and wrapped his arms around the child. "Christian! Look at you!" he exclaimed, his face bright red. Farmer had the wild-looking grin with which he greeted old friends. He turned to me. "This was a terrible case," he said in a low voice, in English.

Nearly two years ago, a doctor from the Children's Hospital had called Socios en Salud and told Bayona, "We have a child here you have to help us with." Christian had already been there for months, weighing only about twenty-two pounds, his lungs filled with TB bacilli and an oxygen mask continually strapped over his mouth. The bacilli had now begun eating his spine and fracturing the long bones of his legs. The Peruvian doctors were following WHO protocol, retreating Christian with standard first-line antibiotics that had failed to stop the TB in the first place. The three-year-old was only getting sicker, wasting away before everyone's eyes, as the mutant germs flourished. When Farmer and his team intervened, proposing a very aggressive combination of MDR drugs—based largely on Farmer's guesswork—they needed official approval from the Peruvian doctors before the drugs could be administered. Farmer confidently told them he had consulted world-renowned experts and read all the literature. All that was true. What he didn't say was that there was nothing concrete in the pediatric literature about treating MDR, and he was basing the dosing only on the drug manufacturer's recommendations, which had nothing to say about children.

The Peruvian doctors gave their consent. The young boy was clearly dying and in agony. Why not try it? Through email, Farmer dutifully kept track of Christian's progress and eventual recovery, but he hadn't seen him or his family until this moment. Despite the damage to his legs from MDR, Christian could actually run! As he waddled around, giggling for the American doctor, Farmer's famous blush spread over his forehead and down his neck, and, I imagined, past his necktie toward his feet. Nothing made him happier than seeing a patient beating all odds to make a recovery.

◆—◆·◆·◆—◆

Christian wasn't the main case Farmer had been asked to consult on today. He was making the hospital visit at Bayona's request, as a favor to a Peruvian TB doctor whose daughter was sick. We were ushered into an office where Farmer introduced himself to a team of local doctors, including the father whose daughter had TB. Her X-rays and CT films were mounted in a viewer for Farmer to study. He checked her records, too, which revealed she had gone through the standard DOTS regimen, only for her TB to resist the antibiotics. Now she was being retreated with the same first-line regimen and, of course, Farmer knew, as he put his stethoscope to her chest, she was only getting sicker.

"This is really terrible," he murmured to me, out of the side of his mouth.

To the girl's father and the other doctors, he spoke in Spanish, reviewing treatment options. Bayona had told Farmer that he was sure the girl's father had known for months she had MDR-TB, but he wasn't about to challenge the WHO protocol, alienating him from his superiors and risking losing his job. In secret he had turned to Bayona, an old friend, and asked—*begged,* Jaime said—to get Farmer to examine his daughter. Bayona had had the girl's sputum cultured and sent everything to the Massachusetts State Lab, quietly bypassing the Peruvian national lab in order to protect his friend from scrutiny. The Massachusetts lab had confirmed the MDR.

Farmer was here today to consult, not dictate, so he diplomatically reviewed the treatment options with the doctors in the room. He finally suggested that a specific second-line therapy *might* be the sensible answer. This of course was his prejudice, he made clear. As in Christian's case, he knew he couldn't step on toes or force his views on anyone, not without offending important people. But what he really wanted to say was "What's the matter with you people?" He knew that his recommended regimen would be the *only* way to save the girl's life. The doctors listened carefully and then expressed their agreement with Farmer—some, like the girl's father, eagerly and gratefully.

Farmer played out the rest of his part. He promised to send his report and recommendations to the father by email. He gave everyone in the room repeated assurances that the girl would be given the best care possible. Finally, with many thank-yous and bowings and scrapings and warmest wishes to their beautiful wives and distinguished husbands, he departed the room.

Soon after, the doctors at the Children's Hospital would put the girl on Farmer's regimen, and she would recover to full health.

CHAPTER 17

IN EARLY 1998, Socios en Salud was treating more than a hundred people with MDR in the northern slums of Lima. The staff had been handling the first fifty-three patients for the better part of two years, with astonishing results. It appeared that more than 85 percent were cured. A friend of Farmer's and Jim's at the Brigham, Howard Hiatt, former dean of the Harvard School of Public Health and now a Harvard Medical School professor, made a suggestion. In April, the same international "TB tribe" of experts—college professors, public health specialists, epidemiologists, and bureaucrats—whom Farmer had addressed in Chicago was convening in Boston at a meeting of the American Academy of Arts and Sciences. Hiatt insisted that Farmer use the meeting to trumpet his latest results, because the Lima cure rate gave significant credibility to Socios en Salud. If the right people knew of the project's success, Hiatt added, PIH might be able to secure new financing for its work.

Farmer and Jim were, among other things, pragmatists who understood that even with Tom White's generosity and PIH's fund-raising efforts, the organization was overextended and sometimes close to being broke. Addressing a prestigious forum couldn't hurt their cause. Farmer also wanted to continue to cultivate a relationship with the head of WHO's TB program, Arata Kochi, whose widely accepted DOTS regimen Farmer had been criticizing for some time, at least for its limitations in treating MDR.

A former student of Hiatt's at the Harvard School of Public Health, Kochi had begun to reexamine his program under the constant pressure from Farmer. He didn't like the bad publicity DOTS was receiving and conceded before the Boston meeting that WHO needed a strategy that included effective MDR treatment. One of his staff had come up with a new, catchy term, "DOTS-plus." Kochi would, in fact, use the phrase in his opening remarks at the meeting.

Farmer and Jim believed that Kochi was conceding not only that DOTS faced limitations in treating MDR but also that bone-eating, organ-devouring tuberculosis was a much bigger problem in the world than many would admit. After Hiatt began the meeting with a keynote speech, Farmer listened to the experts argue, sometimes in heated voices, about MDR and other TB issues. Attendees sat around tables made into giant rectangles with their name cards and cups of coffee or bottled water in front of them, making speeches. For most, their points of view were already well known.

But a bearded Russian named Alex Goldfarb, a rumpled-looking microbiologist, leaned over his microphone and, in his accented English, startled everyone by saying, "So, Russia is a TB nightmare."

Working for the Soros Foundation, a privately funded philanthropy organization, Goldfarb had been focusing on a very specific health crisis—a hundred thousand inmates in Russian prisons with active TB. Most if not all were being treated with only a single drug because the government hadn't come up with the money to buy more. Everyone knew that one drug alone would never stop TB. With very limited funds, Goldfarb was setting up a few DOTS programs in Russian prisons, hoping to stop the disease before it became an epidemic.

"So," he continued, "it is a nightmare. Most of these one hundred thousand inmates will probably die without ever knowing whether they have MDR-TB or not." Goldfarb admitted he didn't have the slightest idea what to do with the MDR cases, which he estimated at 10 percent of those infected. The Soros Foundation wanted to implement an MDR program if there was money for it. But the question would be cost.

He turned to Farmer. "And I would very much like to know, how much drugs did you use for your fifty-three cases and how much did they cost?"

Farmer had already announced his amazing cure rate at the meeting. As Hiatt had hoped, people were impressed. Now Farmer spoke more cautiously. "I'm not saying that it's not expensive. It's been very costly. I'm not saying it's not going to be difficult. But I will say, as Dr. Bayona has suggested, that we have managed to overcome these obstacles for that small number of patients. And that leads me to believe that it would be possible ultimately . . ."

When he finished speaking, much of the talk in the room turned to affordability. A PIH ally said that costs would only rise if the world delayed taking on MDR. Another expert took a different view, essentially saying there wasn't enough money to treat MDR, no matter how encouraging Farmer's results. But a PIH doctor spoke up, saying that he had signed the Hippocratic Oath to practice medicine ethically, but he didn't remember signing an oath to do it in a cost-effective way. That brought scattered applause from the PIH-ers.

Goldfarb spoke again, his voice calm and acidic. "I want to share with you a simple reality. I have six million dollars. With three million dollars I can implement DOTS for five thousand Russian prison inmates. And assuming that ten percent have MDR-TB, forty-five hundred will be cured and five hundred will die from MDR. So I have a choice. And my choice is to use another three million dollars to treat the five hundred with MDR-TB, or go to another region and treat another five thousand. So my choice is not involved in the human rights of five hundred people, but five hundred people versus five thousand people. And this is a very practical question for me, because I have six million dollars. And if I disclose to the Russian people that I spent six thousand dollars per case in MDR-TB in the prisons with tens of thousands of people dying all around, they will tell me I am building a golden palace for a selected few."

There was a great commotion in the room. It was assumed by many PIH allies that Goldfarb had already made up his mind—he wanted his resources to go to curing the vast majority. Hiatt had to bang his gavel to restore quiet. He diplomatically asked Goldfarb if he couldn't use some of the Soros Foundation money, in a pilot project perhaps, to address the question of how MDR affected DOTS.

Hiatt was implying that more research might show Goldfarb how devastating MDR, if left unchecked, could be for the world. He added that Arata Kochi, as head of the TB program for WHO, had come to recognize this threat and had introduced the idea of a DOTS-plus strategy. Indeed, a committee would soon be formed to study the details of such a program, though a cynical Farmer knew that committees were often the graveyard of good ideas.

Goldfarb stubbornly held his ground. "I can't afford

doing a pilot project," he said. "We're not doing a pilot project."

The young PIH-ers glared at Goldfarb. But he'd made an argument that sooner or later they would have to answer. Did one let politics, cost-effectiveness, and limited resources determine the global approach to controlling and treating TB? Or would it be the belief that every life was sacred, and that MDR potentially threatened more lives than any other infectious disease? Maybe the answer was an AMC—area of moral clarity—to Farmer, Bayona, and Kim, but not to everyone in the TB community.

Many argued that nations whose resources weren't just limited but scarce had to make the best possible use of the little they had. If they needed help from wealthy donors or institutions, they had to pass a test called cost-effectiveness analysis. That meant that you calculated the cost of a public health project or medical procedure and tried to quantify its effectiveness. Then you compared the results for competing projects or procedures. Wherever you could get the best results for the least money was what you chose. That was the meaning of cost-effectiveness.

Farmer and Kim made similar calculations when deciding what to do next in Cange. But it seemed to them that certain members of the TB community used cost-effectiveness analysis to rationalize an irrational status quo: MDR treatment was cost-effective in a healthy place like New York but not in a place like Peru, where the standard of living and health conditions were substantially worse.

In the opening speech the next day, Jim Kim said many people had asked him why a small organization like PIH had taken on such a costly and difficult project in Peru. They were right to wonder, he said.

"We actually had to make a choice that we would not feed four thousand more children in Haiti perhaps. And if any of you have been to Haiti, there's hardly anything more morally compelling than the situation of landless peasants in the central plateau."

But, Jim went on, "We took on this project because we thought that by proving that one could do community-based treatment of multi-drug-resistant TB, we might have the opportunity to work with a roomful of people like you. To actually *expand* resources to a problem that afflicts the populations we serve.

"And the only time," he added, "that I hear of *shrinking* resources among people like us, among academics, is when we talk about things that have to do with poor people."

The room seemed to be divided between applause and silence. Undaunted, Jim went on, referring to the Boston meeting as "a TB All-Star Weekend." He suggested that the combined resources of the attendees, using their clout to access research, publicity, and people with money, could be marshaled to defeat the worldwide menace of TB, one project at a time. He insisted that what Socios en Salud had accomplished in Peru could be copied in other places, if there was the political will to do it. Jim was playing not to individual egos but to a common sense of humanity, purpose, and urgency.

"And let me just conclude," he said, "by paraphrasing someone of our tribe, of Paul's tribe and my tribe of anthropologists. Margaret Mead once said, 'Never underestimate the ability of a small group of committed individuals to change the world.'" He paused. "'Indeed, they are the only ones who ever have.'"

CHAPTER 18

KIM, FARMER, AND Bayona had proven that effective MDR treatment was possible, even in a slum in a poor country. Their fifty-three patients were, in effect, a clinical trial, and an astonishingly successful one. TB experts had declared MDR treatment inordinately expensive, but no one had tried to reduce the main expense, which was high-priced drugs. Shortly after the Boston meeting, Jim went to WHO headquarters in Geneva. No one he talked to there even knew that the patents on all but one class of the second-line antibiotics had expired years ago. And no one there seemed very interested when Jim declared, "We can drive down the prices by ninety to ninety-five percent."

Tell everyone you're going to do it, then figure out how you're going to do it—that was Jim's strategy. "The big-shot strategy," Farmer called it approvingly.

◆—◆—◆—◆—◆

Jim had been born in South Korea but grew up in Muscatine, Iowa, in the 1970s. He hardly noticed the Mississippi River flowing by the town, or the rich farmland nearby. His father was Muscatine's periodontist and adapted easily to his new country, liking small-town America. Jim's mother had studied at the Union Theological Seminary under several famous theologians and became a Confucian scholar, ending up for many years a housewife in Muscatine. At every opportunity she took Jim and his siblings to Des Moines and Chicago so they would know that the world was larger than it seemed from Muscatine. She taught her three children the art of debate and tutored them on current events, translating for Jim the images of famine and war that upset him on the TV news. Early on, Jim imagined himself becoming a doctor to treat such suffering, and his excelling in science classes quickened his interest.

He was quarterback on the Muscatine high school football team, a starting guard in basketball, the president of his class and its valedictorian. No matter how much of a leader he was, on a deeper level he discussed with his mother who he really was—Korean or American? The Kims were one of two Asian families in Muscatine, and when they went to the malls of Iowa, Jim was often stared at or made fun of. He felt the isolation that came from being different. When he enrolled at the University of Iowa, he felt liberated from the small-town ways of Muscatine, but not liberated enough. He transferred to an Ivy League school, Brown, where he joined an organization called the Third World Center. As he pursued pre-med studies, he began making friends among African American, Asian, and Hispanic students. He stopped dating white women. Rejecting much of his midwestern upbringing, he embraced the idea of Asian "racial solidarity." Reading for the first time about the internment camps for Japanese Americans during World War II, he went on to lecture about it. He also decided to learn Korean. He got a fellowship to travel to Seoul and happened on an interesting story for his PhD thesis in anthropology—it had to do with the Korean pharmaceutical industry. He made every effort to understand Seoul's culture and to fit in, believing that ethnic identity was the central problem of his life.

By the time he returned from Korea to Harvard, to continue medical school and write his anthropology thesis, he had grown a little bored with what was called, in academic circles, the politics of racial identity. The students and friends he'd hung out with in Korea cared mostly about Korean nationalism or what college they were going to— preferably in the United States—and what degree they would earn. It was all an exercise in selfishness, Jim thought.

By the time he met Farmer as a fellow med student, Jim was ready for a new direction. Farmer told him during their talks in the old one-room PIH office, "If you come to Haiti, I'll show you you're *blan,* as white as any white man." The comment would have offended Jim's friends at Brown, but as he got to know Farmer, to understand his view of the world—to understand the "great epi divide"—it confirmed what Jim was starting to feel: the significant thing was not the color of your skin but whether you were oppressed socially and economically, whether you had access to education, shelter, clean water, and food. It wasn't long before Jim decided that he wanted to make Farmer's preferential option for the poor his own life's work.

All his life, it seemed, Jim had been jumping at the next new thing, the bigger and better thing. Perhaps this was the result of growing up in Muscatine with a cosmopolitan mother who'd always urged her son to live "as if for eternity." Like his mother, Jim had a fondness for drama and overstatement. He'd been talking about "changing the world" long before his speech to the TB tribe in Boston. But in his heart Jim didn't believe it was overstatement. His ability to be totally focused on something, to be committed with determination and enthusiasm, made him a leader. A lot of students had joined PIH after hearing him talk. Change the world? Of course they could. He'd been with the organization for a decade by now and done a lot of its more menial chores along the way. Whatever it took to make a difference. He liked to say of PIH, "People think we're unrealistic. They don't know we're crazy."

<hr/>

From his PhD research on Korean pharmaceutical companies, Jim knew that the price of a drug to the public often had little to do with the costs of manufacturing or distributing it. Often, the price is high because only one company makes it. A firm can secure this monopoly power through patents, but that wasn't the case with the second-line TB drugs. Many of the patents had died. Drug companies didn't care. The potential market was big—worldwide, as many as 750,000 people suffered from MDR, and treating all of them would require a significant quantity of drugs, because treatment lasted so long. But these were largely people who were poor and powerless. Why make drugs for people who couldn't pay? Those companies that did make MDR drugs could pretty much name their own price.

For example, Eli Lilly, one of the world's largest pharmaceutical companies, made the second-line TB drug capreomycin, or "capreo." At the Brigham, Farmer and Jim had to pay $29 a vial for capreo. After repeated badgering by Farmer, Lilly was finally selling it to PIH in Peru for $21 a vial. Then he and Jim discovered the same vial cost only $8.80 in Paris. When they tried to buy it in Paris, a drug company representative told them they couldn't. "There's a global shortage of capreo," he said to Farmer over the phone.

"Why?" Farmer asked.

"There seems to be an emergency."

"Where?"

"In Peru."

Jim went to Howard Hiatt at Harvard. When he heard the story, Hiatt said, "Looks like price gouging to me." In fact, so-called differential pricing was standard in the world of large drug companies; Americans paid more for their products than people in any other country. Hiatt knew someone on the Lilly board of directors and hoped that the company would want to pick up favorable publicity by donating capreo to the project in Peru.

Hiatt and Jim started to work on Lilly, while Jim also tried putting pressure on WHO. He succeeded in getting WHO to agree to sponsor a meeting of drug companies; they would be urged to produce more second-line drugs, and competition would drive down prices, Jim thought. When WHO backed out of its promise, Jim convened his own meeting in Boston. He brought together representatives from multinational drug companies, independent middlemen and distributors, nonprofit organizations—almost anyone who might have an impact on drug pricing. His presentation fell mostly on deaf ears, until a young Dutchman, who worked for a nonprofit company in Holland called International Dispensary Association, grew frustrated at the impasse. IDA specialized in driving down prices of essential drugs, the kind that the indigent sick need most urgently.

"IDA," said the Dutchman at the meeting, "is going to do everything we can to lower prices, by exploring generic manufacturers."

The Dutch group's strategy was to ignore the giant multinational drug companies, the ones that rely on research and brand names and patent protection. Instead, IDA would deal with the many smaller drug companies that make and sell, at greatly reduced prices, already invented drugs, selling them under their generic names (for example, acetaminophen instead of Tylenol). Jim embraced the strategy immediately. His tendency to jump to the latest and greatest idea might be considered a weakness, but in this case he was certain that IDA's plan could serve PIH well.

One of his first tasks was to convince the generic manufacturers that reduced second-line antibiotic prices could still result in significant revenues and profits. They needed to be assured that more TB projects than just Socios en Salud would buy the drugs. Jim went back to WHO, which serves as the coordinating body for virtually all of the world's ministries of health. He began lobbying officials there to include the various second-line antibiotics on their list of "essential drugs"—a list that the ministries followed and allocated money for in their budgets. This would guarantee sales for the drug companies and motivate them to produce the drugs at cheap prices.

Jim immediately ran into resistance in Geneva. To its critics, the World Health Organization was an entangled, muddled bureaucracy that had two mottoes: "Slow down" and "It's not our fault." Jim was told that various eminent TB critics had written to Geneva that they couldn't agree with adding second-line antibiotics to the essential drug list. Some wrote that the plan wouldn't work. Others believed that if it did work and prices fell, the drugs would become *too* widely available. The latter objection had substance, Jim knew. In the real world, many countries lacked even simple health services, and others had clinics and hospitals staffed by the ignorant, the careless, and the lazy. In the real world, some doctors peddled drugs on the black markets, desperate patients sold their antibiotics to buy food, and stupid pharmacists mixed up prescriptions. Start distributing the second-line antibiotics in settings like these and you'd breed resistant strains that no drugs could cure, critics said.

The only way to prevent this kind of mismanagement, Jim thought, was to establish guidelines for sound, well-financed MDR treatment that could be added to the DOTS program. To find a means to ensure real control over cheaper drugs, Jim enlisted the help of an ally at WHO, a young man who had worked at PIH. "See if you can find a precedent," Jim asked of him. The PIH-er called back with the name of an international entity called the Green Light Committee, established to control the distribution of a vaccine for meningitis.

"That's great," Jim told him. "Let's do the same thing. We'll create a committee to control second-line drugs."

"What do we call it?" asked the PIH-er.

"How about Green Light Committee? That'll make it seem like we're just following precedent."

The idea was simple. They would use the same name, but *their* Green Light Committee would serve as the ultimate distributor for second-line TB drugs. Once prices fell, the committee would have real power. TB programs that wanted low prices would have to prove to the committee that they had a good plan and a good underlying DOTS program, one that wouldn't cause further drug resistance. Most of the TB tribe came around to endorsing the idea, and in a final compromise, WHO placed the second-line antibiotics in an annex to its essential drugs list.

The price reductions came in stages. By 2000, TB projects buying through PIH's Green Light Committee paid about 95 percent less for four of the second-line drugs than they would have in 1996, and 84 percent less for the two others—close to Jim's original boast when he had approached WHO about lowering prices. Also, he and Howard Hiatt had persuaded Lilly to donate large amounts of two of the antibiotics to PIH, and Lilly had promised to give other MDR treatment projects vastly lowered prices. "Capreo" now cost just 98 cents a vial, compared to the $29 a vial that the Brigham pharmacy once quoted Farmer. Overall, the drugs to treat a four-drug-resistant case of MDR now cost PIH about $1,500 per patient, instead of $15,000, and prices were still falling. Arguments from the opposition were far from over, but no one could say anymore that cost alone ruled out treating the disease in poor countries.

Jim's "big shot" strategy, as Farmer called it, had worked: dream high, work hard, be open to new, better ideas when they come along, and never, ever give up. To those who knew and worked with him, that was Jim to the core, and it was largely due to his efforts that prices had fallen so much.

CHAPTER 19

———• ·◦· •———

SINCE THE START of the Peru project, Jim and Paul, while in good communication through email and phone, had seen each other infrequently. When they finally met up at a TB meeting in Salzburg, Austria, they went out for a pizza dinner afterward. Jim had a lot on his mind. A few years back, Farmer had talked him into training as an infectious disease specialist. After a few months Jim had quit. He liked doctoring well enough, but Peru had introduced him to medicine on a different scale. It was the big issues surrounding health care—the chance to impact international policy—that excited him. He actually liked sitting for hours in conference rooms talking about operational research in international TB control. But he felt slightly ashamed to admit to Farmer he wanted to have a hand in creating international policy. He worried Paul would think he was just jumping to yet another, bigger idea.

As it sometimes happened, Paul seemed to know what Jim was thinking. "What do you want to do now?" he asked his friend. There was warmth in his question.

Jim was happy for the chance to come clean. "Political work is interesting to me, and it has to be done. It's O for the P on an international scale."

"Well, then do it," Paul said.

"But didn't we always say that people who go into policy make a preferential option for their own ideas?"

"Yeah, but, Jim, we trust you with power. We know you won't betray the poor."

As much as he admired Paul and was influenced by his views, Jim sometimes felt overwhelmed by his friend's self-assurance and charisma. Starting Socios en Salud in Lima was Jim's first major effort to get out of Paul's shadow. Prior to that, he had worked selflessly behind the scenes at PIH, sometimes doing critically important things, sometimes the menial stuff. He used to pick up Farmer from the airport, but Paul never did that for him, not once. When they argued, which happened fairly often, Paul usually came out on top—or if he didn't, Jim felt compelled to make him think that he had. If Jim praised him, Paul was apt to say something like, "Thanks, Jimbo. I need to hear that."

One time, when Jim replied, "Yeah, but why don't you ever say that to me?" Paul seemed surprised. "I do, don't I?"

Jim liked to say that he and Paul were "twin sons of different mothers." If so, Jim had been born second, and now, over pizza in Salzburg, he'd come of age, with Paul's blessing.

A lot of Farmer had rubbed off on Jim. Over the years their philosophical views had become almost identical, including the notion that unrelenting efforts by individuals, if backed with teamwork from organizations and individuals committed to the same goals, could change the international health system. Paul's and Jim's work to lower the per capita cost of health care for the poor was changing the way the world viewed health care; what had once seemed impossible was now possible. As anthropologists, Jim and Paul knew that culture was constantly changing. Practices such as slavery that once had been considered acceptable were no longer morally defensible. Ignoring the poor, Jim and Paul believed, was also morally indefensible, and the world was beginning to recognize that.

In challenging the status quo, one of the arguments the two men always ran up against was "resources are limited." In international health, that argument lay behind most cost-effectiveness analysis. Farmer like to answer that resources were always limited, but medicine now had the tools for stopping many plagues, and no one could ever say there wasn't enough money in the world to pay for them. You just had to get your priorities straight.

At PIH, the organization was facing its own financial crisis. No one wanted to trim its list of priorities, but how to raise funds when Tom White's money eventually ran out was subject to much debate. PIH had spent several million dollars of the philanthropist's fortune to buy the drugs for Peru. Ophelia, in charge of PIH's budget, had managed to set aside about a million dollars from other donors with the hope of forming an endowment, but in the end that money had gone to Peru as well. White was now in his eighties and, as he intended, not far from the end of his fortune.

In early 2000, Ophelia wrote to Paul and Jim that their financial situation was growing desperate. Between the cost of supporting their work in Haiti and Peru and maintaining staff, overhead, and other projects in Boston, White's money was not enough. The three devised what they called a "disassembly strategy"—or, out of earshot of Tom White, "the post-Tom plan." Farmer feared that PIH would be reduced to a tiny private charity, struggling to support its original project in the central plateau of Haiti.

Jim had an alternative vision, of course. Changing cultural values was never a modest undertaking. In Jim's grand plan, PIH would become an instrument for expanding the resources to treat TB, and in the process save itself. They had stopped the spread of MDR in the slums of Lima, and now they would do the same for other parts of Peru. Then they would go international. They would show the world that beating back the dread disease was possible everywhere. And if they could do that with MDR, then why not with AIDS?

For over a year Jim had been courting the "big-shot donors." None was bigger than the Gates Foundation, founded by Bill and Melinda Gates from their Microsoft fortune. The foundation had an endowment of roughly $22 billion, which generated about $1.1 billion in annual income to spend on various projects, about half of it to improve global health. Howard Hiatt had introduced Jim and Farmer to the foundation's senior science adviser, Bill Foege. Foege was one of the people responsible for the eradication of smallpox in the world and was known to favor unconventional solutions to supposedly impossible problems. Jim started putting a grant proposal together. When he met up with Paul again, in Moscow, they talked about how much money to ask for from the Gates Foundation. Paul thought $2 million, maybe $4 million.

"No," said Jim. "We're going to ask for forty-five million."

Paul said they'd never get that much.

Borrowing one of Farmer's famous lines in debate, Jim said, "On what data exactly do you base that statement?"

Part IV

A LIGHT MONTH
FOR TRAVEL

CHAPTER 20

———— ◦•◦ ◦•◦ ————

ONE DAY IN 2000 I met with Howard Hiatt in his Brigham office. He told me, "Paul and Jim had mobilized the TB tribe to accept drug-resistant TB as a soluble problem," but victory over MDR was far from assured. Until Paul and Jim's program took firm hold, Hiatt predicted the number of total TB deaths would climb well above two million. He felt that Farmer, with his communication and political skills, was spending too much time with patients. He needed to devote more of his energies to improving global health policy and practice. TB and AIDS loomed over the new millennium. Malaria and other infectious diseases weren't going away, either. As good as Farmer was as a clinical doctor, Hiatt had been urging him to rethink his priorities, including reducing his Haiti involvement to the role of consultant.

Farmer was forty now, a medical superstar, and he had the credentials to operate in the way Hiatt envisioned, the way that Jim Kim liked to operate—on an executive level. But he wasn't ready to abandon clinical practice, certainly not in Haiti, where he had worked for almost two decades. It wasn't that he didn't want to do all he could to cure the world of poverty and disease. He just had his own ideas on how to go about it. Individual patients always came first. Then he made time for everything else. In 2000, he was receiving about seventy-five emails a day and answered the vast majority: consults on MDR patients in Peru; ideas for PIH projects in Russia, Mexico, Guatemala, and Roxbury; and requests for advice from around the world from priests and nuns, anthropologists, health bureaucrats, and fellow doctors. There were also requests for counsel and letters of recommendation from former PIH-ers who wanted to attend medical school, young doctors and epidemiologists who had enlisted in the PIH cause, and a specialist in Boston who sought Farmer's advice on the care of an indigent HIV patient.

When he was away from Haiti, he was flooded with Creole emails. One came when he was in Miami, on the way back to Haiti, from a Zanmi Lasante staffer.

"Dear Polo, we are so glad we will see you in a mere

matter of hours. We miss you. We miss you as the dry, cracked earth misses the rain."

"After thirty-six hours?" Farmer said to his computer screen. "Haitians, man. They're totally over the top. My kind of people."

Early in 2000, I tagged along with Farmer on what he called "a light month for travel." We had spent two weeks in Cange, and in the midst of them had taken a quick trip to visit the church group in South Carolina that funded Père Lafontant's projects. Now we were heading to Cuba for an AIDS conference. We'd spend the week after that in Moscow on TB business, with a stop in Paris en route.

When he was younger, Farmer had traveled to and from Cange in jeans and a T-shirt, until he realized this upset his Haitian friends, who always dressed up to travel. Then Père Lafontant told him that if he was going to represent them to the world, he should wear a suit. Farmer owned two but had lent one to a friend. The one he kept was black, which seemed to hide some of the inevitable wrinkles that came with travel, so he could arrive at his destination looking somewhat presentable.

On the morning we left for the Port-au-Prince airport, on our way to Havana via Miami, Farmer was in his suit. He insisted, as usual, on driving the Zanmi Lasante truck himself. He suffered from motion sickness, and being at the wheel lessened his nausea. He issued last-minute instructions to staff, and when ten people had crammed themselves into the cab or the bed of the pickup, needing a ride to various destinations, we departed the complex.

It was six a.m. We hadn't eaten breakfast. As we lurched down National Highway 3, my back felt wrenched already. This road of endless ruts and missing stretches of pavement had been built during the first American occupation of Haiti, in the early twentieth century. The U.S. Marines had supervised its construction, forcing peasants to do the labor. When those in the central plateau staged a rebellion—refusing to be treated as slaves—their insurrection was put down violently by Marine-supervised Haitian police, not unlike the French masters had done to their ancestors. In a book Farmer had once shown me was a photograph of a defiant road worker; the man lies on the ground with both hands cut off.

I was narrating Haiti on my own, in my mind, as I looked out the windshield. The past seemed to blend seamlessly with the present. The view of emaciated beggars and barefoot children lugging containers of water never changed much. I saw a thin man in a straw hat on a starving Haitian pony, kicking the animal's protruding ribs, hurrying, I imagined, to get to work on some infertile piece of farmland so his children could have at least one meal today. I began searching my mind for a consoling way to view the roadside sights and also, frankly, for something likely to impress Farmer. Remembering my religious education, I said to him, "If you've done it unto the least of them, you've done it unto me."

"Matthew twenty-five," Farmer picked up. "'Inasmuch as you have done it unto the least of these my brethren, you have done it unto me.'" He went on, paraphrasing. "'When I was hungry, you fed me. When I was thirsty, you gave me something to drink. When I was a stranger, you took me in. When I was naked, you gave me clothes. . . .' *Then* it says, 'Inasmuch as you did it *not,* you're screwed.'" He smiled, swerving around another giant rut in the road.

Our conversation wandered. Farmer was concentrating on negotiating the narrow, winding highway, with its dangerous blind spots. Ahead, we suddenly spotted a truck turned onto its side, not far from where Paul and Ophelia had come upon the dead mango lady seventeen years before. This time there were no people around the wreck, no bodies on the ground. Someone in our truck was sure the accident had something to do with a curse. Farmer translated this for me and laughed and, still laughing, drove on.

Our first stop was a jail in a Port-au-Prince suburb. An unchecked *bwat* on Famer's list of things to do read "Prison extraction." One of our passengers, a peasant farmer, had a son, Michela, who was being held on suspicion of murder. Farmer had already arranged for a lawyer. He was stopping at the jail so the father could speak to his son. Inside, the cell where the young man languished was unlit. There were at least thirty men in the shadows, crowded together, and a fierce stench was wafting out at us. The son stood at the bars and talked to his father. Farmer passed on the news to the boy about the lawyer, delivering hope amid all the squalor.

Back in our truck, Farmer said to me, " 'When I was sick, when I was in prison, when I needed clothes, you gave me,' et cetera. We got those covered." He went on, "One thing that comes back to me, with all this cost-efficacy crap, if I saved one patient in my whole life, that wouldn't be too bad. What did you do with your life? I saved Michela, got a guy out of jail. So I'm lucky." He added, "To have a chance to save a zillion of them, I dig that."

After an errand downtown we reached the airport. The traffic was snarled as usual. Crowds always thronged the airport when a big plane was coming or going, and most of the people seemed to have no business there except hope. It wasn't just taxi drivers looking for fares who gathered at this seam in the world but children and old men and women leaning on sticks and people with missing limbs, all straining at the barriers, shouting and waving at the arriving passengers.

As we boarded our plane, I was relieved to be going, but Farmer always found it hard to leave Haiti. "You and I, we can leave whenever we want. But most Haitians are never going to get to go anywhere, you know?" he said. A little later, when the plane banked over the Bay of Port-au-Prince, he glanced out the window once, then turned his face away. When the central plateau came into view, a brown landscape dotted with just a little green, eroded mountainsides, and rivers turned murky from topsoil washed away by rain, Farmer narrated Haiti for what would be the last time in a while. "It bothers me to even look at it. It can't support ten million people, and there they are. There they are, kidnapped from West Africa."

He got to work, writing thank-you notes to PIH contributors. Finishing five, he mentally checked off a *bwat,* which cheered him. But his mood was volatile that day. He could easily lapse into self-criticism, particularly if there was someone, especially a child, whose life he thought he could have saved in Cange. He referred to a little girl who had died the night before, one he felt shouldn't have. He'd stayed up all night, trying every trick he knew to keep her alive. This was the first I'd heard of it. I told him I was sorry.

Ophelia thought that Paul's personality was built of oppositions—a need for frenzied activity that verged, she thought, on desperation, and a towering self-confidence oddly combined with a hunger for affirmation. He was always asking, "How am I doin'?" and if she didn't praise him, he'd be hurt. She thought that she understood; he took on more than he could fix, so of course he wanted reassurance. And yet he also seemed "terribly simple." She didn't think he had even experienced true depression, despite the grimness of his surroundings and what would seem to others to be insurmountable obstacles. "I've never known despair and I don't think I ever will," he wrote to me once. It was as if in seeking out suffering in some of the world's most desperate locales, he made himself immune to the emotional pain that came more typically to the rest of us. He was often sad, of course, but it didn't take much to cheer him up.

When we landed in Miami, Farmer surveyed the cabin. He identified about 20 percent of the passengers whom he guessed had never flown before—the very thin ones, the ones with callused hands and faces, the men who looked self-consciously dressed up, the women in dresses that were covered with ruffles. "We're about to see something horrible," he said.

"What?"

"The escalators."

He stood near the top of the first. Every fourth or fifth Haitian would come to a stop at the head of the escalator and look down at the moving stairs. They'd pause as if at the edge of deep water, and then start down the escalator, running, trying to match the apparent speed of the stairs. "Don't run. Hold on to the rail," Farmer called in Creole to an elderly-looking woman about to tip over. She regained her balance. He turned to me, his face grim again. "The more ruffles, the more stumbles." He told me he'd spoken to airport authorities about the problem, but evidently they hadn't listened.

We drifted through the Miami airport. This was his usual hub. Many business travelers rated it as one of their least favorite airports, but Farmer loved layovers here. He could get a haircut from his favorite Cuban barber and then take a hot shower and hang out in the Admirals' Club, a benefit for those with lots of frequent flyer miles. He'd answer emails from a soft easy chair while sipping red wine. Because our flight to Cuba wasn't until the next morning, we stayed overnight at the airport hotel. Between flight cancellations and Farmer suddenly changing his mind about where he was going and for how long, his travel schedule required constant monitoring—a task that fell on the shoulders of his brand-new assistant at PIH. She had complained that she joined the organization to do social justice work, not to be a travel agent. The young woman deserved some sympathy. No one had ever been able to keep Farmer's schedule flawlessly. His last assistant had come close to perfection, but he had ended up promoting her.

That night in our room, Farmer smashed his toe into a suitcase in the dark. By morning, the toe had turned purple and he diagnosed a fracture. He managed to limp along through the terminal without complaint, his computer bag over his shoulder, a plastic shopping bag in one hand, and his suitcase in the other. The latter was packed minimally with changes of clothes—only three shirts for two weeks—because it was too full of other things, such as slides for his upcoming lectures and presents for his Cuban hosts. It seemed that Farmer could never bring enough gifts wherever he traveled, whether because someone in Haiti asked him to deliver a package to a relative in the States—he rarely said no because he didn't like to turn anyone down—or because he was speaking somewhere and wanted to properly thank his hosts. He had so many gifts for his Cuban hosts that they couldn't all fit in his bag. I put the extra presents in my suitcase; Farmer was very grateful.

I remarked on his sleepless nights, his hundred-hour weeks, and his incessant travel as he hobbled along.

He said, "The problem is, if I don't work this hard, someone will die who doesn't have to. That sounds megalomaniacal. I wouldn't have said that to you before I'd taken you to Haiti and you had seen that it was manifestly true."

Up ahead, we could see the check-in point for our Havana charter flight. You could tell from the piles of luggage, the boxes containing radios and kitchen appliances, the sacks full of things like disposable diapers. What Cubans couldn't buy in Cuba—unless it was on the black market, and that was usually expensive—had to be brought in from abroad. The scene resembled the ticket counters that served flights to Haiti, or to any other poor country in the world.

Farmer was smiling, and I figured he was looking forward to Cuba, because he said, "No dead babies for a while."

CHAPTER 21

WHEN OUR PLANE descended toward Havana, Farmer grew excited as he peered out the window. "Look! Only ninety miles from Haiti, and look! Trees! Crops! It's all so verdant. At the height of the dry season! The same ecology as Haiti's, and look!"

The Cuban doctor who had organized the AIDS conference, Jorge Pérez, was a short man in his mid-fifties, an old friend of Farmer's. He had sent a car for us. Pérez held numerous important positions. He was chief doctor of Cuba's Infectious Disease Institute, chair of the national AIDS program, visiting professor in many countries, and a member of the board of directors of one of Farmer's Harvard programs. On our ride into Havana, I got my first glimpse of a political billboard, an enlarged version of the famous photograph of the Marxist revolutionary Che Guevara wearing a beret. Che had served as a military adviser to Fidel Castro when Castro and his guerilla army overthrew Cuba's former president, Fulgencio Batista, in the 1950s. Later, Che was killed in Bolivia while trying to lead a rebel army against the government. He was a martyr and a hero to Castro and most Cubans.

After Castro took power in 1959, the United States broke off diplomatic relations with Cuba. Trade between the two countries ceased. It was the middle of the Cold War, and the Soviet Union opportunistically filled the void we left by providing money, supplies, and technical support to the new government. If you were an American citizen, it was illegal in most cases to visit Cuba from the United States, but permission was granted for international conferences like this. Farmer had visited before. He was fond of Cuba, not, I thought, for its political system or ideology, but mainly because of its remarkable health statistics.

According to WHO, life expectancies in Cuba were about the same as in the United States. Diseases that plagued Haiti ninety miles away, including AIDS and TB, were rare and under control here. In a population of about eleven million, the country boasted more doctors per capita than any other country in the world, and twice as many per capita as the United States. It was a poor country, in part because the United States maintained its trade embargo, and because the Soviet Union, once it collapsed in the late eighties, no longer provided financial subsidies. Yet its public health system allowed all Cubans virtually free medical care. Hospital equipment was not always the most up-to-date, but WHO regarded Cuba's doctors as well trained, and the government, proud of its reputation in public health, sent many of them abroad to work in other poor countries, including Haiti.

Farmer admired Castro for protecting the sick and the vulnerable, for the way he managed the country's poverty. Farmer didn't believe in Marxism, but he was impressed, as I was, by just how much a country with little in the way of natural resources could accomplish. After enduring too many trips on Highway 3, I was relieved to find that most roads around Havana were paved. While the cars were mostly older American models (dating to the time before Castro) or Russian ones, they seemed to be in decent shape, and a source of pride for their owners. Cuba had food rationing but no starvation, no enforced malnutrition. Housing projects were in need of repair, but compared to the slums of Port-au-Prince, Cuba looked lovely to me.

When we got to our hotel, Farmer said, "I can sleep here. Everyone here has a doctor." He lay down on his bed and quickly fell asleep.

When he woke, refreshed, he admitted that he relished a break from his routine in Haiti. Yet in Havana his schedule could hardly be called restful. He was scheduled to give two lectures. With the help of Dr. Pérez, he also hoped to raise money for Zanmi Lasante from people he didn't yet know. His priority was to stockpile antiretroviral drugs—enough, for starters, to treat twenty-five patients in Cange who had full-blown AIDS.

As the conference kicked off, Farmer met a woman named Peggy McAvoy, who was in charge of the United Nations' project on HIV/AIDS for the Caribbean. He lobbied her for several days, even inscribing a copy of his book, *Infections and Inequalities,* "For Peggy McAvoy with a big hug of solidarity and with high hopes for your help in Haiti." With a little encouragement from Dr. Pérez, who approached Peggy and told her that Farmer was a friend of his, she finally relented. She asked Farmer for a written proposal. He now had a foot in the door. He said to me on the side, "No one gives guilt trips like I give."

Another of Farmer's hopes was to begin to solve one of Zanmi Lasante's most persistent problems. All but one of the Haitian doctors who worked in Cange had their homes in Port-au-Prince or abroad. They were middle-class Haitians, Farmer said, adding that they regarded living in Cange as living in the sticks. There was nothing to do, many claimed, but work and play table tennis—Farmer had recently bought the doctors a Ping-Pong table—so after being trained by Doktè Paul for a year or two, they usually left. Farmer wanted to begin creating doctors who were

Cangeois, people who were born and lived in Cange. He and his staff had picked out two local youths whom he hoped to send to the new medical school that Cuba was opening for Latin American students.

When Farmer told Dr. Pérez of his plan, his friend arranged a meeting between Farmer and the secretary of Cuba's Council of State, a distinguished-looking doctor whose nickname was Choumy. They talked for a while, and then in Spanish Farmer asked Choumy, "Can I send you two students this year?"

"From the U.S.?"

"No, Haiti."

"*Por supuesto,*" he answered. "Of course."

Luc Montagnier, the French doctor generally credited with discovering the HIV virus, was speaking at the conference. The French ambassador to Cuba also showed up. When the three got together, Farmer told them, in French, that he dreamed of a new kind of "triangle"—doctors from Cuba and money from France coming together in Haiti. By using the word *new,* Farmer was playing on the term *triangular trade,* the trade that had created the French slave colony that eventually became Haiti. After some hesitation, Montagnier accepted Farmer's invitation to visit Cange and Zanmi Lasante. The ambassador told Farmer, "Yes, we, too, are going to help with the Haitians."

Farmer, it was clear to me, knew how to work a conference. The promises he got from various doctors and dignitaries, whether they were kept or not, were a testimony to his charm and persistence, and would be followed up with Farmer's calls, letters, and emails. If they didn't bring results, they still might produce a little shame, which might increase the chances that the next promise would be kept.

Of the two talks Farmer was scheduled to deliver, one was for clinicians about the specifics of treating AIDS, and the other was more general, about poverty and inequality, especially in Haiti. He delivered the second in the amphitheater at Cuba's infectious disease hospital, where on a screen he showed a color side of the blue waters of the Péligre reservoir, deceptive waters to anyone who knew the history behind them. Farmer loved telling the story. "Now, in this country where I have worked for eighteen years," he began, "the *campesinos* [peasants] lost their land to a hydroelectric dam."

The hydroelectric dam began a tragic turn of events for all the peasants, but especially for the women of the central plateau, Farmer said from the podium. As the HIV/AIDS epidemic spread around the world, and a wave of fear and superstition with it, Haitians were quickly labeled a "risk group." It was as if the world thought Haiti was heavily populated by intravenous drug users, homosexuals, and the sexually promiscuous. Farmer, the anthropologist, designed his own study centered on a random group of about two hundred women in Cange. He found that the peasants' vocabulary didn't even have a word for illicit drugs, which almost no one could afford anyway. None of the women had been sexually promiscuous; on average they'd had sexual relations with two different men, consecutively, not concurrently. Of those women who were infected with AIDS, many had contracted the disease in Port-au-Prince. In a country with a 70-percent unemployment rate, the capital offered the most opportunities for work, often as servants for the wealthy. But the long hours and meager wages meant the need for additional income. Desperation, deep poverty, and illiteracy drove women to take the risk of cohabiting with men such as truck drivers and soldiers, those with steady jobs or who wielded the power of intimidation.

After his study was done, Farmer returned to the States and did additional research. When he entered the search term "AIDS" into a computer, thousands of studies came up. When he entered "AIDS and women," only a handful of studies appeared. "And when I crossed 'AIDS, women, and poverty,'" he told his audience, "the message said, 'There are no studies meeting those specifications.'"

The screen behind him filled with an enlarged graph of the Cange study. He told everybody that if they wanted to stop AIDS, they needed to look closer at countries such as Haiti. They would find that places with the steepest grades of inequality and the greatest poverty had the biggest AIDS problems. "We need to erase social inequalities, and very few countries have done that," Farmer spoke up. He closed in one of his favorite ways, by quoting a peasant: "You want to stop HIV in women? Give them jobs."

By now I was getting a sense of how Farmer put together experience and philosophy. In trying to control TB and AIDS in the central plateau, he didn't dwell on third-world myths, such as beliefs in sorcery, but chose to challenge first-world ones, such as so-called expert theories that exaggerated the power poor women had to protect themselves from AIDS. The poor needed education, jobs, and decent housing.

When he finished his speech, the amphitheater, about half full, give him a long, loud round of applause. This was Cuba, of course, a third-world country that was trying to give its citizens the very things Farmer talked about. But he was prepared, too, to take his message to the less sympathetic, more prosperous nations.

CHAPTER 22

———— ·—·—·—· ————

FARMER TOLD ME he'd like to hang out at the conference, to meet people and to spread his message about disease and inequality, but he spent less time there than in our hotel room. He typed on his computer until his eyes shut from exhaustion, only to suddenly jump up and begin pacing the room, swinging his arms, giving himself a pep talk: "Come on, Pel. Come on." There were numerous grant proposals to write, and a piece on MDR-TB in Russia. He was also working on his new book, *Pathologies of Power,* of which he had a completed first draft.

The book contained a chapter on the two ways AIDS had been managed on the island of Cuba after the disease became a global threat in the early 1980s. Both involved quarantines—the practice of isolating someone with a highly infectious disease from the healthy population.

Castro's regime had responded one way, sending those with HIV to a hacienda about an hour's drive from Havana. The hacienda served as a sanitorium—a medical facility for those with long-term illness—and Dr. Pérez was in charge. The patients were a combustible mixture of infected soldiers and homosexual men. A military presence ensured that order was maintained and that no one could leave, though everyone was well fed and received proper medical treatment.

The second way was the American quarantine in the early 1990s of HIV-positive Haitian refugees, who were detained at the United States naval base at Guantánamo Bay. Under the 1903 Cuban-American treaty, Guantánamo Bay, on the southeast corner of the island, was under permanent control of the United States. Part of the base had served as a military prison over the years. While the HIV-infected Haitians had committed no crime, they were nevertheless treated like prisoners. According to Haitians who survived the ordeal, they lived in isolation and were forced by U.S. soldiers to eat tainted food and were subject to harassment, including beatings. Eventually an American federal judge ruled the quarantine unconstitutional and ended the Guantánamo program.

Farmer strongly believed that quarantines were not an effective strategy for handling AIDS, but the Cuban approach had been far more humane. The hacienda accommodations had electricity and running water. When the government felt that AIDS was no longer spreading on the island, patients at the hacienda were allowed visitors, and temporary passes if they could be trusted to practice safe sex. Ultimately the quarantine was lifted altogether. Pérez had expected everybody to leave at that point, but 80 percent stayed behind, as living conditions at the sanitorium were better than in other parts of Cuba.

One day, Dr. Pérez picked us up at our hotel in his battered Russian sedan and we drove to the hacienda, in a place called Santiago de las Vegas. I enjoyed looking at the countryside, all colored for me by contrast with Haiti's— the electric power wires, the irrigated fields. As Dr. Pérez's driver turned onto the hacienda grounds, we passed a bare-chested, heavily muscled young man wearing a black beret and riding a bicycle. Farmer asked the driver to please stop. He jumped out and called to the man, "Eduardo!" Eduardo did a double take, climbed off his bike, and, approaching Farmer, greeted him with a heartfelt hug. Grinning, they were quickly engaged in conversation. I would learn that Eduardo was a former Cuban solider who had contracted AIDS and been a patient here, treated by Dr. Pérez. On a previous trip to Cuba, Farmer had also doctored Eduardo. I never heard Farmer complain of having too many patients, and it seemed clear that he couldn't feel comfortable anywhere not having any at all. So in Cuba he borrowed some from Pérez. The opportunity was reciprocated. When

Pérez came to Boston, I learned, he liked to go on rounds with Farmer.

Farmer climbed back in the car, and we continued on to the hacienda, once owned by a wealthy family that had fled the country when Castro came to power. The interior had high ceilings and many rooms. Stains darkened the walls here and there. It was worn at the edges, but not exactly shabby, and still an active sanitorium. Dr. Pérez led us on a tour of the patients' quarters, including little houses and apartments set among gardens and palm trees. We visited Eduardo's modest house. On the bureau was a snapshot of Farmer. When Paul spotted it, his face turned red. Recovering, he said to Eduardo, "I see you're still smoking cigarettes." Eduardo offered him the pack, and Farmer pushed it aside, laughing. "No. I was about to say you should quit."

When the tour resumed, Farmer kept remarking on how pleasant and peaceful the quarters were, and finally I said to him, "I find them kind of depressing."

"Really?" He seemed surprised. "Compared to what I grew up in, it's pretty nice. They have gas stoves, air-conditioning, electricity, TV." Actually, it wasn't the sanitorium's housing that troubled me. I felt that Farmer was suspending his usual critical judgment, looking only for things to praise. So I was doing the opposite. Maybe I just wanted an argument. He clearly didn't. He let the subject drop.

As we walked the grounds, listening to Dr. Pérez, I was impressed by what Cuba had done about AIDS. It wasn't fair to compare Cuba to the United States—they were too different in size and complexity—but by 2000, despite an overall drop in HIV and AIDS cases in the United States, those diseases had claimed a much larger percentage of the population than in Cuba. Meanwhile, Cuba had the lowest per capita incidence of HIV in the Western Hemisphere, following Castro's program of mandatory HIV testing for nearly everyone, and a successful effort to clean up the blood supply at hospitals. In 2000, only 2,669 people had tested positive for HIV. The virus had progressed to AIDS in 1,003 of those people, and 653 had died.

We drove back to our Havana hotel. One evening Farmer and I went to dinner at Pérez's house, which was as large and well-furnished as a unit in a decent American housing development. Farmer made sure I noticed that Pérez's driver ate with the family. Another night, we dined with Pérez at a restaurant rumored to have been one of Ernest Hemingway's favorites when the American writer lived in Cuba. Men with guitars came up and serenaded our table. Farmer seemed delighted. Almost everything he encountered in Cuba—including, at our hotel, the variety of fish in the ponds, whose species he could easily name, and the caged cockatoos in the lobby—pleased him

Cuba really was a holiday, by Farmer's standards. Because of poor connectivity on the island, it was impossible to access email—he'd pay for this later in catching up on correspondence—so he actually had free time. I thought he might want to see the sights of Havana, but that required the ability to relax. Wherever he traveled in the world, he rarely took time to enjoy the local culture or history, such as Machu Picchu in Peru or the Bolshoi Ballet in Moscow. It was as if Farmer had built himself an alarm system that, with any extended free moment, set off a recording saying, "You're forgetting Haiti."

He stared out at a magnificent banyan tree along a route that Pérez's driver took, and said softly, "I've worked for eighteen years in Haiti, and everything has gotten worse."

"What about Zanmi Lasante?" I said at one point.

"Zanmi Lasante *is* an oasis, the best thing of its kind in Haiti. But it's not as good as here. The Cubans would have done a better job."

I was listening to the Farmer who honestly believed that he could never do enough. When he combined that attitude with a righteous indignation about how the world treated the poor, his conviction was hard to ignore. People took notice of what he had to say, and in turn Farmer seemed to marvel at the attention he got. Pérez, who was an important and busy man in his country, continually chose to spend time with Farmer rather than other dignitaries at the conference. Back at our hotel, Farmer asked me why I thought people made such a fuss over him. I said that I imagined the Cubans liked his published attacks on American policy in Latin America, his admiration of Cuban public health and medicine, and his efforts to create connections between Cuba and Harvard. "And Jorge constantly introduces you by saying, 'He is my friend.'"

My comments must have struck Farmer as a put-down, because when I looked across the room his pale blue eyes were fixed on me. The Farmer stare. It could make you think he was examining an X-ray of your soul or, if you were irritated with him, that he imagined he was examining one. My eyes wanted to look away, and I wasn't going to let them.

"I get the same reception everywhere," he said. "I'm stupefied by the way the Russians receive me, and I hate their wacky system. Why is it the same across all these radically different settings? I think it's because of Haiti. I think it's because I serve the poor. *Love, ID.*"

I had the impression he was angry, disappointed, and a little hurt, and that I was in the doghouse for my lack of understanding. But it was also typical of Farmer that he couldn't stay angry or upset for too long. "Whatchya thinkin' over there?" he said minutes later as I was reading a book on my bed. I felt I was forgiven, and though I wasn't sure for what, this was a relief.

It didn't last.

With the conference over, we waited at the Havana airport for our plane to Miami, where we would connect to a flight to Paris and a visit with his wife, Didi, and their young daughter, Catherine. The Miami connection was delayed, so we passed time in an airport restaurant. For a while Farmer joked in Spanish with the server, and then the conversation turned to the book I was writing. Farmer started by asking what I was going to say about Che Guevara. "If you're going to write about Che," he said, "it should be your opinion. Not mine."

"Why is that?" I asked.

He was giving me the stare. We soon got to the heart of the matter: what really concerned Farmer was what I would write about *him* in Cuba. He was afraid I would paint him as a sentimentalist or, worse, some spineless ally of the Cuban government. He was afraid that I would interpret all the attention that Cubans gave him as his reward for being an unofficial spokesman of Castro's socialist government. Farmer made clear this was far from the truth, and that underneath the fondness he felt for many things Cuban, at his essence he was "a hard-bitten, clinic-building, MDR-treating mother."

He gave me something of a lecture. He didn't care about his personal reputation if I chose to portray him inaccurately, he said, but he did care greatly about the harm any inaccuracy might do to his credibility in the medical world. If his work was cast in the light of politics and propaganda, this would harm his mission, and thus his patients, not to mention the efforts of Pérez and other Cuban doctors to assist their poor. Like Pérez, Farmer didn't like social inequality. He believed in social justice medicine. He championed a preferential option for the poor. And he didn't want to see his beliefs mischaracterized or his work ridiculed in the book I was writing.

There was vehemence in his voice, and I felt I was its object, as if I had already ridiculed Dr. Pérez. I knew how warm and giving Farmer could be. I had seen him cry over patients and the memories of patients. He greeted everyone in his circle with blushing elation. I, too, had enjoyed basking in that warmth, grateful for it, yet at this moment I felt a definite chill. Was he saying he'd rather not travel with me anymore? Well, then, the feeling was mutual. I was getting weary of his constant righteousness and the sense I was in some way a great disappointment to him.

Then he changed subjects. He announced we would be going to Russia next. He said it wasn't as important as Haiti.

"Well, do you think I shouldn't come along with you?" I said. I tried to make my tone nonchalant. I'm not sure I succeeded.

He looked surprised. "No, no. It's important."

The scolding, if that's what it was, ended there. Farmer had his own way of explaining our uncomfortable exchange. He said our conversation had been the "dismount" of our time in Cuba. He had borrowed the word from gymnastics, in which his sister Peggy had once competed, and he used it often with doctors at the Brigham. "Okay, let's do the dismount," he would say, and they'd wrap up the discussion of a case.

After our "dismount," it was hard to stay angry at

Farmer as we boarded the plane to Miami. When we reached our destination, it was quite late, but Farmer eagerly, and no doubt with some anxiety, opened his computer. More than a thousand unanswered emails were waiting, including many about patients. As he figured out which ones to answer first, my thoughts turned to my book. I didn't think we had much of an argument over Cuba. For Farmer, Cuba represented hope, proof that a poor country could achieve good public health. "If I could turn Haiti into Cuba, I'd do it in a minute," he had said earlier. No matter what I might have thought about the lack of political freedom under Castro, I couldn't deny what Dr. Pérez and others had accomplished, and I readily understood Farmer's frustration every time he looked at Haiti.

As we settled into our seats for a late-night flight to Paris, my stomach began to act up. For the last day and a half I'd suffered from diarrhea, the result of drinking too many mojitos, deceptively strong rum drinks, in Cuban restaurants. I was determined not to complain to Farmer—he had enough to deal with—but I did anyway. About to fall asleep, he came to life and looked at me with concern. "From now on," he said, his face utterly serious, "I want a full report on all of your bowel movements."

Farmer wasn't put on earth to make anyone feel comfortable, except for those lucky enough to be his patients, and for the moment I had become one of those. I felt greatly reassured—much better already, in fact—and the last remnants of my anger at him seeped away.

CHAPTER 23

———— ·•+ + +•· ————

IN PARIS, OUR cab let us off in the Marais district, a place
of narrow streets and sidewalks, of bistros, shops, and small
hotels. The Farmer family residence was an apartment of
three small rooms, borrowed from an old friend from
Duke. Didi—tall and stately—met us at the door with an
enormous smile. I was tired from our flight, and my memories of that morning are hazy. But I remember thinking
that Didi probably *was* the most beautiful woman from
Cange, and that their toddler, Catherine, as Farmer embraced her to his chest and did a loopy, long-limbed waltz
in the living room, made him deliriously happy.

After their wedding, Farmer had brought Didi to Paris
because he thought that, like him, she would find the city

the most enchanting in the world, and a comfortable and exciting place to live. Didi's reaction was more ambiguous. She agreed they would establish a residence here, but she was aware of the city's dubious past beneath its splendid architecture, culture, and history. France was responsible for her ancestors' suffering. For a while now she had been examining the archives documenting the lives of French slave masters and their commerce in West Africa. Since then, some of the city's charm had worn off for Farmer.

As we settled in the living room and Farmer watched Catherine play with her stuffed animals, Didi called to him from the kitchen. When was he leaving for Moscow?

Tomorrow morning, he answered.

From the kitchen came the sound of something dropping and a deep-throated exclamation. Farmer remained on the couch, uncharacteristically paralyzed. He was stopping in Paris for Catherine's second birthday—a party had been planned—but he didn't seem to have anticipated his wife's reaction to so short a visit, visits that came all too infrequently in the eyes of his many friends. He counseled others to take vacations but enjoyed few himself, even if that created the impression that his family was not his highest priority. From the way Farmer showed off photos of his wife and daughter wherever he traveled, I knew that he loved them deeply. But I also knew, from other comments he made, that he felt guilty if he couldn't love the sick and dying babies of poor women he barely knew as much as he loved little Catherine. He was full of empathy for the whole world. He saw that almost as a moral responsibility. If taking care of the poor and the sick meant sacrificing time with his family, it was a price he had to pay.

I thought about this for a while before I asked him delicately, "Some people would say, 'Where do you get off thinking you're different from everyone and can love the children of others as much as your own?' What would you say to that?"

"Look," he replied, "all the great religious traditions of the world say, 'Love thy neighbor as thyself.' My answer is 'I'm sorry, I can't, but I'm gonna keep on trying.'"

I knew that some people talked behind his back. "Can you imagine what it's like being married to him?" they might ask. They seemed to think they had found someone who had a chink in his moral armor. That might have made those who were envious of him feel better, but I doubted that they understood Farmer. Guilt and feelings of inadequacy could consume him. He certainly had a gift for guilt-tripping others, but he saved a lot of it for himself. I don't think anyone who knew how much Farmer craved connections among all parts of his life could have looked at him at that moment on the couch in Paris, all folded up as if trying to hide, and not felt sympathy for his predicament.

His difficult moment with Didi passed. That afternoon, Catherine's birthday party was attended by many friends, French, Haitian, and African, including current and former PIH-ers. Farmer thrived on the energy of the crowd. It seemed as if he could never have enough friends; new ones were added to the old until it felt like this special family would never stop growing, wouldn't be allowed to. The party was a success, and Catherine clapped her hands at her present, a mechanical bird on a wire that flew around the living room. Before he went to bed, Farmer called his mother, Ginny, in Florida to say hello. Before hanging up he asked her to give him a wake-up call at seven a.m. Paris time. That meant she would have to make the call at one a.m. from the States. Didi shook her head. "We have an alarm clock," she said to me, but she was smiling.

Some months later, when I was talking to Ginny, she remembered Paul's call and said, "I just think it's so cool that at forty he still does that. I'd miss it if he didn't."

◄ ◆ ► ◆ ►

The next morning, early for our plane to Moscow, we had breakfast at an airport café. Farmer was refreshed and ready to get to work, starting with tackling his most recent *bwat* list. Only about two-thirds of the little boxes on his sheets of paper had been checked. One unchecked matter was an unfinished letter he had started when we'd taken a hike in Haiti. He pulled the letter from his briefcase, ignoring the grease stain on the paper, and picked up his narrative where he'd left off.

"Is this *bwat* transfer or *bwat* cheating?" I asked him.

"Depends on whether or not you have an H of G for the endeavor," he said without looking up.

In Farmer's personal dictionary, "H of G" was short-hand for "hermeneutic of generosity," which he had defined for me in an email as, essentially, always giving someone who is a good person the benefit of the doubt. He was giving himself the benefit of the doubt for why he hadn't finished the letter, as the Cuba conference and other projects had interrupted his correspondence. In addition to "H of G," "ID," "WL," and "O for the P," Farmer used scores of other abbreviations and slang in his daily speech and emails. Jim and Ophelia had invented some of the lexicon, and the expressions had filtered into the PIH culture. One Farmer favorite, using "Hate-ans" or "Hats" for the word *Haitians,* originated when his brother Jeff wrote *Hatians* by mistake in a letter. Farmer liked to refer to himself as "white trash," because he had an old photo of his family at a picnic around a couch outdoors. "Rooskies" were Russians, a "chatterjee" was a person of East Indian descent who talked a lot (there were a few at PIH), "TBMI" stood for transnational bureaucrats managing inequality, and "shaftedness" and "hose-edness" were used to describe the different degrees of how the poor were abused. To commit "a seven-three" was to use seven words when three would do, and a "ninety-nine one hundred" meant quitting on a nearly completed job.

The terms could seem impolite to an outsider, but they reflected Farmer's sense of humor, his quick mind, and his prejudice for brevity. Committing "a seven-three" was what bureaucrats did. Friends called Farmer a word gymnast, which he didn't deny. I thought what he did with language was part of his charm and charisma. His diction could be so contagious that even non-PIH-ers, especially when in his company, adopted the same phrases.

PIH was its own special place, rising from humble origins, when Jim, Paul, and Ophelia used to debate important issues in a shabby office that sat over a Boston restaurant, to a world-strong organization of committed individuals. You could hang around the inner circle of PIH for a long time without understanding what the rules were and feeling excluded, and the more left out you felt, the more you suspected you were being told you weren't as good as they were. To me, however, the inner circle of PIH seemed like a club, or even a family, which was deeply opposed to the concept of insiders and outsiders. Farmer called it "the most inclusive damn club in the world, being full of people with AIDS, WLs galore, tons of students, church ladies, and lots of patients, and it's a club that grows and never shrinks." Yet Farmer had that special gift to make you feel he was creating a club that consisted just of him and you.

As we ate breakfast, Farmer went on writing his letter. Glancing around, I was aware of the disconnect between Farmer's world and the world of gift shops with luxury goods, affluent passengers, and the freedom for some to move about the world without restriction. When I mentioned the disconnect to Farmer, he looked up and said in a chirpy-sounding voice that I was wrong.

"There is no relation between the massive accumulation of wealth in one part of the world and abject misery in another." He looked at me. He'd made me laugh. "You know I'm being funny about something serious," he said.

He often caught me off guard with his humor, and it seemed to relax him to make me and others laugh. He could quote lines from his favorite comedies, like *Caddyshack,* or poke fun at someone who was too pretentious or willfully ignorant. When Farmer was being serious, however, the core of his being was exposed and he wanted you to pay close attention. Once I listened to him give a talk on HIV to a class at the Harvard School of Public Health, and he mentioned the Haitian phrase "looking for life, destroying life." Then he explained, "It's an expression Haitians use if a poor woman selling mangoes falls off a truck and dies." I felt at that moment I could see a little way into his mind. It was a place of hyperconnectivity. I thought what he wanted was to erase both time and geography, connecting all parts of his life and tying them to a world in which he saw intimate, inescapable connections between the gleaming corporate offices of Paris and New York and a legless man lying on the mud floor of a hut in the remotest part of remote Haiti. Of all the world's errors, he seemed to feel, the most fundamental was the "erasing" of people, the "hiding away" of suffering.

Interconnectedness was not just a feeling and philosophy for Farmer, but something he acted on, in Haiti for sure, but everywhere else, too. One day on an airplane, he confided to me that he thought of all our fellow passengers as potential patients. An attendant's voice had said over the intercom, "Is there a doctor aboard?" Farmer had gotten up at once and attended to a middle-aged man who thought he was having a heart attack but fortunately wasn't. Returning to his seat afterward, Farmer said this happened to him about once in every eighteen flights. I had the impression that he wouldn't have minded if it happened every flight.

Embracing a continuity and interconnectedness that excluded no one seemed like another of Farmer's peculiar liberties. It came with a lot of burdens, of course, but it also freed Farmer from the efforts that many people make to find refuge and distinction from their pasts, and from the mass of their fellow human beings.

CHAPTER 24

———◆—◆·◆——

ON OUR FLIGHT to Moscow, Farmer told me that the World Bank was planning to make a loan to Russia to help prevent a full-blown TB epidemic. This was his fifth trip to Moscow, and now was the time, after countless phone calls, emails, and meetings, finally to secure the loan. Farmer's involvement in Russia had started two years earlier, when he made a futile effort to convince the Soros Foundation to provide funds for PIH's TB work in Peru. The director applauded what PIH was doing, but the foundation had already committed $13 million to pilot projects throughout Russia, where TB was deemed to be a more serious problem than in Lima.

Farmer began paying closer attention to Russia, to wherever there was the specter of a possible epidemic. So far the Soros Foundation had provided funds only for a WHO-approved DOTS program. No money was made available for treating MDR, yet drug-resistant strains were infecting an increasing percentage of the prison population. Those who contracted MDR were left to die—as humanely as possible, because the foundation provided money for hospice care—but why, Farmer wondered, couldn't some money be allocated to MDR? He'd already demonstrated in Peru that treating MDR with only a DOTS protocol made the disease worse in those patients, and he feared that if MDR ever got out of control, it was possible new strains would evolve for which there were no known drugs.

Now Russia was reaching a tipping point. The collapse of the Soviet Union had meant the deterioration of its public health policy. A failing TB control system had led to many uncompleted therapies; rising crime had led to overcrowded prisons. It would have been one thing if all MDR prisoners had died while incarcerated, but many got released after serving their sentences. Infected, they mingled with the civilian population and threatened to start an epidemic.

Farmer had written the Soros Foundation a terse letter stating why their DOTS-only regimen was bound to fail. He ended up in George Soros's Manhattan office, where he compellingly made his case. The billionaire investor/

philanthropist immediately phoned Alex Goldfarb, the Russian microbiologist and head of the Soros Foundation's TB program in Russia. At an earlier international TB conference, Goldfarb had made it clear that with limited funds, he wasn't about to spend them on MDR. Soros yelled at him on the phone. Then he asked Farmer and PIH to help fix the Russian pilot projects.

Farmer wavered briefly. Getting involved with Russia would mean even more weeks away from Haiti. Still, he reasoned that PIH could use some of Soros's money to pay salaries. Besides, Russia's epidemic was ravaging its prisons, and prisoners were part of PIH's special constituency—just check with Matthew 25 if you had any doubts. And Russia would represent the kind of opportunity Paul and Jim had hoped for when they'd taken on Peru: a chance to affect health policy for the poor on a global scale. Russia bordered twelve other countries these days, and some of those countries bordered some of the world's wealthiest. Russian TB might show the world the consequences of neglecting the health of poor people everywhere.

At first, Farmer and Alex Goldfarb, each entrenched in his point of view, didn't get along. But after a tour they took together of prisons in Siberia—the vast region of central and eastern Russia stretching from the Ural Mountains to the Pacific Ocean—Goldfarb had a better understanding of Farmer and MDR. They returned from Siberia as friends. What really united them was what they witnessed in the network of prisons, where TB was now the leading cause of death. Farmer and Goldfarb flew to New York for an emergency meeting with Soros and asked the philanthropist for more funding for Russia. To gain a foothold against the disease could cost hundreds of millions, they estimated. Soros wanted to involve the international community, particularly the United States. He arranged meetings for Farmer and Goldfarb in Washington, D.C., including one at the White House with the First Lady, Hillary Clinton. In the end, Clinton prevailed on the World Bank to give Russia a loan. Farmer had been frustrated by the World Bank's layers of bureaucracy, but he and a PIH team had done everything asked of them, including putting together a 293-page report, commissioned by Soros, that detailed how to create a proper TB treatment program in a country that, at 6.5 million square miles, was the largest in the world. Farmer also agreed to serve as a consultant on TB in Russian prisons for the World Bank's mission to Moscow.

Deplaning in Moscow, we drifted into the main airport, which had all the charm of a warehouse. Outside, the January air was freezing. In the distance we could see the colorful, onion-topped towers of St. Basil's Cathedral, one of the world's most beautiful buildings, Farmer thought, but marred by the fact that Ivan the Terrible had built it to celebrate his bloody victory over the Tartars. Not many in the Russian government liked to talk about their country's unpleasant past. Erasing history, Farmer liked to say, served the interests of power.

The next morning, we joined up with Goldfarb, who had flown in from New York, and some Soros Foundation advisers and Russian officials to visit Moscow's immense central prison, Matrosskaya Tishina. Goldfarb looked like a professor with his beard, his slight stoop, his tweed and corduroy. Besides working for the Soros Foundation, he represented the Russian Ministry of Justice, which ran the country's prisons. Entering Matrosskaya Tishina, I found a confusing maze of cell blocks, low doorways, endless tunnels, dingy corridors, and ancient metal staircases. The air-conditioning and heating were unreliable, and pungent smells sometimes wafted toward us unexpectedly. Farmer had been to the prison before, but an official still warned us, "Don't get lost. This is not a good place to get lost."

We passed a file of inmates, all dressed in baggy pants, ragged coats, and caps, gray faces in dim light; one had one of the most crooked noses I'd ever seen. Finally we reached the prison hospital. "Think of Cuba," Farmer whispered to me in an ironic tone. Russian doctors and health officials—male and female—all wore olive drab uniforms. One opened a door to a cell reserved for inmates with AIDS. There were fifty men, most of them young, clustered in the dingy gray chamber. Farmer went in first, followed by a translator. The space was smaller than many American living rooms, and jammed with double-decker beds and a few clothes-lines. The men gathered around Farmer, airing their grievances about the Soviet justice system, which they accused of giving longer sentences to anyone who had HIV or AIDS.

"You should go to the courts and stand up for the rights for the AIDS-infected on trial," one man said through the translator.

Farmer said he would pass on the information to the World Bank's AIDS specialist. Before leaving, he shook hands with many of the prisoners, rubbing shoulders in the cramped space. It was clear his visit lifted the morale of many of the prisoners, and some asked him to come back again.

"I would like to," he answered.

As we left, the heavy metal door clanged shut behind us, an eerie sound that echoed down the corridor. It wasn't hard to imagine the hopelessness the inmates felt. In Russia at the time, a man could be thrown in jail for stealing a loaf of bread, then languish in a detention center for up to four years before his trial began. While waiting or serving his sentence, he'd probably get infected with TB—it was estimated that 80 percent of all Russian prisoners had bacilli in their bodies. Some died of the disease before they received their sentences.

We were led through another twisting passage before arriving at the TB department: a series of cells crowded with infected inmates. In all of Russia, it was estimated, a hundred thousand prisoners had TB, and thirty thousand had MDR. At Matrosskaya Tishina, about five hundred were infected, and deliberately isolated from the rest of the population. In a complicated logistics system, infected prisoners were sent to Moscow from as far away as Siberia—with stops, it could be a month-long journey—and there was no way to maintain treatment en route. It was also impossible to know how many innocent people picked up the bacteria from the prisoners on these stops. In terms of a spreading epidemic, Farmer and Goldfarb knew this was a nightmare.

We went into a humid cell overcrowded with sick, coughing men. I was struck by the different, distinctive coughs—bass, baritone, and tenor. The humidity came from many pairs of lungs exhaling. Farmer stood beside a bed, his arm resting on the mattress of an upper berth. "You look good," he said to one of the men. "Anybody coughing up blood?"

"No."

"So pretty much people are getting better?"

"It's not getting worse," said a prisoner.

When it was time to leave, Farmer shook some hands and said to the translator, "Tell them I hope everybody gets better."

We headed back to the central prison office. Despite Farmer being upbeat with the prisoners, and the heroic efforts of the Russian medical staff, he and Goldfarb knew things were not getting better. Farmer said to me, "They have seven hundred hospital beds in this place, and about five hundred are filled with TB patients. That's a clue, just a clue, that there might be a problem." On top of the MDR problem, Farmer had learned that the incidence of syphilis in the prison was rising. Alarming, because rising syphilis announces the arrival of AIDS, which would greatly magnify the TB epidemic. "It's gonna be a disaster," Farmer said.

We were ushered into a mustard-colored office where Russian doctors, health specialists, and government leaders were waiting for us. A crude conference table was piled high with food and vodka. Farmer hated vodka but now he cheerfully drank it, just as in Haiti, at a peasant's home, he consumed the unrecognizable dishes offered him—what Farmer called "the fifth food group"—so he wouldn't offend anyone. After many toasts and greetings, Farmer told his Russian hosts about his experience dealing with TB in Haiti and then Peru—how he had relied upon the TB lab in Massachusetts to culture the sputum of sick patients who he suspected had MDR. He emphasized the critical importance of good lab work to determine which drugs to use for which patient. One of the Russian woman doctors spoke up: "We have lots of TB and no labs." Farmer had earlier gotten laughs when he said that in America there were lots of labs and no TB. Underneath any joking, the reality for Russians was alarming. Their prison hospital X-ray machines were in a decrepit state, and there was a chronic shortage of even first-line antibiotics. Money was desperately needed.

To keep up with his hosts, Farmer kept drinking vodka.

A Russian colonel, holding up his pack of cigarettes, inquired of Farmer if America was a democracy. Turning very serious, Farmer answered with a long speech about democracy and socialism, the rich and poor, power and privilege. Finally Goldfarb made a face, stopping Farmer. He explained that the colonel only wanted to know if he needed permission from Farmer to smoke his cigarette, if that was what happened in a democracy. "But the speech was marvelous," added the colonel, smiling at the American doctor. Farmer suddenly looked so exhausted from the alcohol and his talking that he seemed on the verge of falling asleep.

"Tomorrow," Goldfarb said, turning to the colonel, "Paul will represent your interests at the World Bank."

Farmer shook himself alert. "The only thing wrong, I don't think it should be a loan. But for the international community of healers it will be a good thing. I pray"—he put his hands together in a steeple—"that it will go well."

———◆•▸•———

At the meeting the next day, and at several that followed, the course of events was anything but smooth. In the world of TB control, experts were still fighting about MDR treatment. There was finally consensus that with lower prices from generic drug companies for second-line antibiotics, MDR could be treated cost-effectively. The World Bank was ready to loan money to Russia for both DOTS and

DOTS-plus programs. What was in dispute was how much money the prisons would receive and how much would go to the civilian sector. Farmer and Goldfarb were allies in wanting as much as possible for treating inmates. However, World Bank members, who came from many countries to meet in Moscow, were divided about the allocation. One reason, Farmer learned at a cocktail party, was Alex Goldfarb. A certain World Bank official implied that Alex's brashness and outspokenness turned off many people. He was hurting Farmer's cause. Even though Goldfarb represented the Russian Ministry of Justice, which ran the prisons, Farmer was warned explicitly to keep Alex away from the meetings.

When Farmer told Alex what the official had said, he was outraged. "Who is this? I am so amazed by him. Such arrogance and ignorance."

Farmer tried to reason with Alex, but the Russian wasn't pacified. Goldfarb went on, "The World Bank brought here an expert with a turban from India, and he doesn't know anything about Russia. These people don't know what is going on with this country. The people you are meeting with are totally insignificant."

Farmer reminded Goldfarb of their mutual objective, to get as much money as possible for the prisons, and not to get defensive about personalities. Alex continued with his attack, not just on members of the World Bank but on the World Health Organization bureaucrats stationed in Moscow, who he said resented PIH and the Soros Foundation. Adding to the complexity and jealousy, according to Alex, the Soros Foundation itself contained competing factions with different points of view about Russia. Also, he said, some of the local WHO bureaucrats were Polish, not Russian, and between the two nationalities old hatreds still endured.

Alex reveled in all this conflict, I thought. I could understand why he was perceived as an agitator by some World Bank members. Then Alex began talking about the rivalry between the Ministry of Health and the Ministry of Justice. The Ministry of Health, in charge of TB control in the civilian sector, wanted most of the loan. Alex, speaking for the Ministry of Justice, insisted that the prisons were the core problem; they had over half of the TB cases in Russia and certainly most of the drug-resistant ones. If you didn't stop the epidemic in the prisons, he said, any lasting accomplishments with the outside population would be questionable. In the end, the World Bank members decided that the Ministry of Justice—the prisons—would get only 20 percent of the loan. Most of the money would go to the Ministry of Health.

Farmer sympathized with the needs of the Ministry of Health, but he still hoped that the loan could be divided fifty-fifty. Alex, frustrated and angered by the World Bank's decision, decided at one point that everything should go to the Ministry of Health. He reasoned that the resulting chaos in TB control would reach catastrophic levels, and finally private foundations would have to step in and deal with the prisons. Farmer was having difficulty communicating with Alex, who wouldn't accept anyone's point of view but his own. Farmer seemed to say that diplomacy, charm, and sound argument backed by hard data could unite all factions against their common enemy, TB.

As the meetings in Moscow continued, Farmer looked as if he was enjoying them less and less. Jim Kim had the finesse and diplomatic skills to deal with bureaucrats and large organizations such as WHO and the World Bank. Farmer was a diplomat, too, but he often lacked Jim's patience. And there was so much on his mind: his patients and friends back in Cange, his family in Paris, his work with PIH, the papers and books he was writing—and always the important emails waiting on his computer. As I looked at him in his permanently rumpled black suit, part of his hair sticking up like a rooster's, his frustration and fatigue showing in his face, I worried for him. One evening, after he had received an email that quoted a World Bank team member as saying, "It's ridiculous and too expensive, this proposal for the prisons. It's ridiculous," Paul suddenly found himself thinking like Alex. Over breakfast with me the next morning, he said, "I'm trying to keep myself from slugging the guy."

But he kept his composure that day and continued with his diplomatic approach. When the Russian negotiating team reminded everyone that Paul Farmer warned of a looming TB epidemic, and that he was one of the most respected epidemiologists in the world, the World Bank finally seemed to listen. It was agreed that the prisons would get about half of the loan after all. The first installment was projected to be $30 million, and ultimately the Ministry of Justice expected to receive another $100 million. A large part of the monies would fund a pilot project in Tomsk, Siberia.

When Farmer met Alex at their hotel that night with the good news, Goldfarb was finally happy, or as happy as he could be. He was cynical enough to always find something to worry about. Yet his respect for Farmer, despite their differences, was beyond doubt.

Farmer in turn said about Alex, "Only a mother could love him. I do love him. I really do. And this whole thing in Russia is going to work. You know why? Because he loves me."

They seemed to have the sort of friendship that thrives on argument. Whether it was Cuba, Russia, or the United States, whether about the nature of crime, money, or bureaucracies—or human nature in general, including how many people really belonged in prison—their views rarely matched. If it were up to Farmer, I thought, he would immediately pardon over half of the inmates he'd visited, maybe all of them, whereas Alex insisted that 25 percent should be locked up for the rest of their lives. We had dinner together that night, consuming three bottles of wine, and then Farmer and I trudged back to our hotel in the biting cold, his red scarf covering his nose, his glasses fogging up.

I said, "You look thinner than when we started out."

"It's been a long trip,"

I couldn't argue. I wondered how many more "light months for travel" he could endure. At the moment he was philosophical. He would do whatever it took to accomplish his mission.

"Do you think I'm crazy?" Farmer asked, referring to his argument with Alex about pardoning prisoners.

"No. But some of those prisoners have done terrible things. . . ."

"I know," he said.

"But you forgive everyone."

"I guess I do. Do you think that's crazy?"

"No," I said. "But I think it's a fight you can't win."

"That's all right. I'm prepared for defeat."

"But there are the small victories," I said.

"Yes! And I love them!"

My thoughts were a bit hazy, and I sensed my voice was a little slurred. I began to pose a hypothetical question, which I thought expressed insight into Farmer's itinerant, nomadic life. "You're a great guy," I said, putting a hand on his shoulder. "But without your clinical practice—"

He interrupted. He said, "I wouldn't be anything."

Part V

O FOR THE P

CHAPTER 25

In July 2000 the Gates Foundation gave Partners in Health and a cohort of other organizations $45 million—virtually everything Jim Kim had asked for—to wipe out MDR-TB in Peru. The money, in the form of a five-year grant, would be funneled through Harvard Medical School. Because Gates would give only one grant, Jim made peace with PIH's potential or former adversaries, such as WHO's tuberculosis branch, who would otherwise be competing for the grant. In short order everybody agreed to work under one umbrella—PIH. In the next five years, Jim calculated, they'd have to treat about two thousand chronic MDR patients and cure at least 80 percent. If successful, the

Peru program would prove to the world that countrywide control of MDR was possible.

In scaling up a community health project such as Socios en Salud into a national one, Jim and Paul faced many challenges. One was keeping overhead under control. PIH traditionally used only about 5 percent of its donations for administration, with 95 percent going to patient care. Many nonprofits consumed 20 to 25 percent of their donations for overhead. Requests from PIH staff to be paid for working extra hours "because other institutions did it" were rebutted by Farmer. He would say, "One can never work overtime for the poor." Ophelia managed to finesse the situation, giving overtime where required by law and dealing with other people on an individual basis. She simply didn't tell Paul.

Another challenge for Jim and Paul was to remain in close contact with core PIH backers. No one should think that support from the Gates Foundation, or grants from other foundations, relieved donors of the need to keep giving. Along with its sister organizations—in Chiapas, in Roxbury, in Haiti—PIH couldn't succeed without ongoing funding from thousands of individuals, particularly since Tom White's money was running out. Farmer's campaign to expand AIDS treatment in Haiti was especially costly.

The PIH staff was also mushrooming. When I first visited their headquarters in late 1999, about 20 people worked for the organization. Now there were 50, plus another 10 in

Roxbury. The numbers in Haiti had grown to about 400, and to 120 in Peru, and PIH was about to inherit 15 employees in Russia, which included a presence in Siberia as well as Moscow. The new, expanded headquarters in Boston, donated by Harvard Medical School, now housed specialists in grant writing, technology, and administration in addition to regular staff.

As much as Farmer wanted to direct the PIH spotlight away from himself, he was known to drop in on the new headquarters like a mini-hurricane, commanding everyone's attention. He might stay for only twenty-four hours, leaving for the airport the next morning, but he immediately got busy asking questions of staffers, giving assignments, making everyone run off in various directions on some important errand. He was always polite, but his expectations for others in the organization were high, Ophelia told me. For those left in the wake of the hurricane, Farmer's brief, intense flurry of activity could result in a case of nervous exhaustion—a case of "decompressing from Paul," Jim said.

But Farmer wouldn't or couldn't slow down. There were too many demands on him. On the Russian front, after helping secure the World Bank loan, he received a special request from the Soros Foundation. It was growing unhappy with Alex Goldfarb for the political melodramas he was staging within Russia, which were angering the government and making Goldfarb ineffective for the foundation. Soros wanted PIH to take over the project in Tomsk, Siberia. One of the oldest cities in Siberia, with a population of half a million, Tomsk, and the huge territory around it, had a serious MDR problem. Tomsk was to be *the* major pilot project to stop the Russian TB epidemic, the project that would show the way to controlling—in prisons, towns, and cities throughout Russia—both drug-susceptible TB and MDR.

After much deliberation and discussions with Soros, Farmer and Jim agreed to take on Tomsk. It was a risky bet. If they weren't successful, PIH's critics would claim that AIDS and TB could never be treated successfully in impoverished areas, and years of PIH work would come into question. The good news was that the World Bank loan would provide for staff and medicine. However, someone had to be in charge of the effort on the ground. Originally, Paul had agreed to fill the clinical role if Jim would assume the managerial role and most of the diplomacy. Both men were already stretched thin with other commitments, and Jim suddenly seemed to be backtracking on his promise to attend an important banquet and press conference in Tomsk.

"*You* said yes to Russia," Paul told Jim at a Cambridge restaurant where Ophelia and I joined them for dinner. After an initial exchange of pleasantries, Farmer's voice had changed. It was intense and rising. "You promised me! And you're not gonna go!"

Jim protested calmly. He had another TB meeting in

Bellagio, Italy, with the Rockefeller Foundation. He would get to Tomsk afterward. Farmer's face turned red. The veins in his neck stuck out. He told his friend that Bellagio could wait. It was critical that Jim go to Tomsk *now*, for the press conference. Farmer, looking to Ophelia for support, kept badgering Jim. "You won't do it, I know it, you're going to cancel, you won't go. Look," Farmer added, "I would like to go to my *grave* never having gone to Bellagio."

He turned to Ophelia. "I'm asking him to limit the damage in Russia."

She said softly, "He knows that, P.J."

"Well?" said Farmer. "Force him to do it."

Jim turned to Ophelia. "He's trying to irritate me enough . . ."

"I know," she said.

Farmer had told me in Cuba that no one could give a guilt trip like he could. The tension at the table didn't ease. Ophelia didn't seem to mind that she was stuck in the middle. I learned later that she had seen far more ferocious arguments between the two. She once said that Paul never let himself lose his temper when it might jeopardize PIH's mission, but I saw tonight that he might lose it to make a mission happen. After a while the explosion had run its course, and we settled into enjoying our meal. When the evening was over, Jim and Paul walked out the door together, Paul with his arm around Jim's shoulder and Jim with his arm around Paul's, and I could see they were laughing. A few weeks later, Jim flew to Siberia, as Farmer had wanted. Jim invited me along.

·—◄·•·►—·

It was four hours by plane from Moscow to Tomsk. The Siberian city had several huge public buildings, monuments from World War II, a reputable university and medical school, and some factories that provided decent jobs. Yet there was an air of decay. The old wooden houses looked lopsided on their foundations after decades of long winters; yards were full of junk poking out of the snow. When Tomsk Air had gone bankrupt, it greatly reduced the number of flights into the city, and with the reduction came a slowdown in visitors and businessmen. And the city water, because of recent flooding, wasn't safe to drink when we got there.

Jim and I had arrived just in time for a banquet honoring the project. In front of Russian television cameras, the vice minister of justice, in charge of Russia's prisons, would announce PIH's new role in Tomsk. Farmer was supposed to be there as well, but he was stuck in Paris due to a delay in getting a visa. The event took place in a small, luxurious private hotel. In addition to the vice minister of justice, Russian doctors, dignitaries from other health organizations, and ten Russian generals in olive drab uniforms sat on one side of the assembled tables. These men were in charge of administering the prisons on a day-to-day basis.

Farmer had made friends with many of them during his tours of the prisons, and everyone knew the TB project couldn't succeed without their support. But they had never met Jim, and even after the normal toasts were made, vodka glasses raised high, Jim felt they didn't trust him, not without Farmer around.

Spying a TV equipped for karaoke, he made a bold announcement as he raised yet another shot of vodka to the generals. "I'm a terrible singer, but in my culture, Korean culture, if you respect someone and you have a deep affection and admiration for the people you're with, you should embarrass yourself by singing for them. So I will sing for you." Jim then belted out "My Way" on the karaoke machine as the words scrolled across the TV screen. When the equipment abruptly malfunctioned, Jim went on alone, hitting a few sour notes. Everyone clapped, and then other guests followed by singing their favorite songs, including a two-star Russian general who chose a hit from Russian TV. Even the vice minister of justice insisted on performing, and his was the best voice of all. Soon people were dancing. By the end of the evening, with the jailers of Russia joined together in song and dance, I don't think I merely imagined, even with the late hour and the amount of vodka consumed, that the farewell speeches were tinged with affection.

"Dear friends," one general began. "I really mean you are my friends." Bottoms up again. "We just want to do something good for this earth," offered another general. "That we finish this work according to the DOTS program."

Outside, snowflakes lit the air. Jim had managed to turn potential disaster into something affirmative. As he watched the generals depart in a cavalcade of cars, he smiled softly and we returned to our hotel.

The next day, Jim left and Farmer arrived. Paul stayed only one day, which he spent examining MDR patients and giving television press conferences with the vice minister of justice. In the evening, he and I attended another banquet with the generals and dignitaries. The toasts began right away, including one to Alex Goldfarb, from the vice minister of justice, for Alex's hard work and sincerity. Farmer raised his glass in support of Alex, adding, "May he stay out of trouble." A man with tousled hair and squinty eyes appeared. A translator explained he was part owner of the hotel as well as a local oligarch who controlled Siberian gas and oil fields. Drinking heavily, he stood and toasted the virtues of Tomsk.

"Dear guests, I would like to say a few words. Energy is the force of life. Tomsk has oil, coal."

"Bravo!" called one of the generals.

"To the energy program!" cried Farmer from the other end of the table. "I love Siberia!"

He made lots of money, the oligarch added, and he invested some of it in culture and medicine for the city.

Other conversations resumed around the oligarch, who was now clearly drunk. He seemed to be talking to himself about how hard life was in Russia, and then he lurched out of the room. Our dinner was followed by farewell toasts and goodbyes as the generals and dignitaries drifted to the hotel lobby. Farmer graciously thanked the vice minister for all that he'd done. The oligarch reappeared, this time naked except for a towel wrapped around his waist. He headed toward the billiards room, stumbling past the vice minister, who smiled and shrugged and went back to saying his goodbyes. The alarmed hotel manager, a woman in high heels, came running through the lobby, pursuing the oligarch. Farmer, smiling gleefully, turned and watched the chase.

We flew to Paris the next day. In the plane we talked about the Russians, among other things. "I have to say, Rooskies are my kind of people," Farmer announced.

"I've heard you say that before."

"PIH-ers accuse me of saying it about everyone. But it comes in handy in my line of work. To like people."

Then he began the dismount of our short stay in Tomsk. The essence was a review of the drug situation. Low-cost second-line antibiotics would soon be on their way to Russia, but at the moment the supply chain wasn't working. Other organizations, now intent on treating MDR in Russia, were still waiting for the inexpensive drugs. Jim and Paul, by contrast, had asked Tom White for $150,000 and bought enough drugs, at high prices, to start treating a few dozen Tomsk patients right away. Farmer was aware of what his critics would say: why blow $150,000 on antibiotics that, if you'd waited a while, would have cost you a fraction of that? Farmer's answer was that project managers could afford to wait for lower prices, but not all patients could.

CHAPTER 26

FARMER WAS ON the road more than ever, to Peru and Siberia (including one trip all the way from Haiti to Tomsk for a two-hour meeting, which he considered a great success), to Paris (where he'd agreed to give a prestigious lecture series, so as to spend more time with Didi and Catherine), and to New York (where he testified on behalf of a Haitian with AIDS who was at risk of being deported). He went to dozens of American and Canadian universities and colleges, preaching his preferential-option-for-the-poor gospel, and to South Africa, where he debated a World Bank official at an international AIDS conference. He went to Guatemala to see some bodies dug up. (Partners in Health had found a donor to pay for a mental health project there: the digging up and proper reburial of Mayan Indians who had been slaughtered by the Guatemalan army and dumped in mass graves.) One time, not long after he'd taken a fall in Cange and broken both an arm and his tailbone, he flew all the way around the world, bound for Asia on TB business.

I kept in touch with Farmer by email—he wrote almost every day—and sometimes in person. When he returned to Boston for one of his month-long tours at the Brigham, I followed him on a couple of memorable cases. One was a migrant worker from Mexico who had been shipped to Boston from a Maine hospital, suffering from Fournier's gangrene—a skin-eating infection of the soft tissues of the male genitalia. Many staff thought it was time to call in hospice care for the man, but Farmer insisted cheerily, "He's going to walk out of here." About a month later he did. Another case involved a male graduate student who arrived at the Brigham near death. "Toxic shock," Farmer said, correcting the house staff's diagnosis, and quickly adjusted the man's medication. For two weeks he lay in bed delirious with fever, his teeth chattering, the tips of his fingers and toes black. Farmer told his parents to keep hope, because their son was going to be fine in the end. And he was.

Services at the Brigham made life easier for Farmer. The hospital's equipment, staff, and resources were always available to him, without Farmer having to worry about raising money to pay for anything. Yet Boston was hardly a rest. Wherever he was in the world treating patients, he saw as many as he could. There were few free hours. He was still wearing the same wrinkled black suit, which now looked like something from a trash barrel; he couldn't even find time to buy a new one, despite repeated requests from Ophelia.

Keeping up with Farmer by email was sometimes frustrating because he didn't always identify where he was. The one certainty was that he would always end up in his beloved Haiti. Some friends and allies, including Howard Hiatt, felt Farmer should be spending more of his time on worldwide health campaigns, much less in clinical practice. But when Hiatt visited Zanmi Lasante for the first time, he was moved more deeply by it than by anything he'd ever seen before, he told me. He wrote in an article for the *New York Times,* "I have just returned from a health center in a country at the bottom of the economic heap. . . . HIV infections are controlled as effectively in an area of Haiti as in Boston, Massachusetts. . . . Medical care there is delivered with skill and caring comparable to that seen in a Boston teaching hospital."

Cange had always been a special sanctuary for Farmer, and part of him wanted to keep it that way. The central plateau was his roots as an epidemiologist and a clinician, and a model of how a committed staff on a limited budget could raise the standard of health in the third world. In an impoverished rural area, it was the only clinic that gave patients expert care and treatment regardless of their ability to pay. In August 2001, when Farmer published an article in the British medical journal the *Lancet* describing the AIDS treatment and prevention program in Cange, things changed. PIH was flooded with requests for advice and information, from ministries of health and consultants and charities from every continent, about creating such a program in their backyards.

By winter 2002, Zanmi Lasante had to become a laboratory for the world, a template of what could be re-created in a thousand different places, if the war on poverty and infectious diseases was to ratchet up. The catchphrase at PIH became "replicability and sustainability." This could only be accomplished if large foundations and international agencies became more involved. The economist Jeffrey Sachs, an expert on world hunger, visited Zanmi Lasante after reading the *Lancet* article. As Howard Hiatt had done, Sachs began talking to influential individuals and institutions about using Farmer's clinic as a world model.

Sachs had already started an organization called the Global Fund, financed by governments and foundations, with the hope of raising billions of dollars to fight AIDS, malaria, and TB. PIH applied for a grant for Haiti and was approved. According to the plan, Zanmi Lasante would direct an AIDS treatment and prevention program through most of the thousand square miles of the central plateau. It was hoped the project would be a model for similar projects in Haiti's eight other departments and in other chronically poor countries.

After inevitable bureaucratic infighting and logistics problems, the Global Fund money—$14 million for the central plateau, spread over five years—became available. Farmer was so elated, he told me, that he felt like weeping. He vowed to spend more time in Haiti to oversee the expanded project. That would mean, of course, cutting back on some of his international travel, yet a few weeks later he was back in Tomsk, visiting TB patients and checking out the Russian programs. Then it was on to Spain for an international AIDS conference, and afterward a multitude of other commitments. Once, arriving back in Boston exhausted, he confided to Ophelia that he heard two sets of voices. One was that of friends and allies urging him to concentrate on the big issues of world health; the other was the voice of Haiti, saying, "My child is dying." I doubted he was capable of choosing one over the other, even though he talked about retiring one day in Cange so he could be just a "country doctor." It seemed to me that he didn't have a plan for his life so much as he had a pattern. He was like a compass, with one leg swinging around the globe and the other planted in Haiti.

CHAPTER 27

ONE REASON FARMER could never convince himself to choose one path over another was his fundamental dream—an unwavering passion—for equality in health care. That people living, say, in Boston probably enjoyed medical treatment superior to what was available to anyone born in Cange spoke to the heart of "the great epi divide." The unfairness angered Farmer, and he tried to save as many lives as he could in his clinical practice. It grounded him to live in the everyday reality of poverty. Yet he was never going to level the playing field by working only in the central plateau, or in Tomsk, or in Lima. He had to reach out to the global pharmaceutical companies, to governments, to foundations, and educate them that all lives had equal value. Matthew 25 and O for the P were his guiding principles, and he found it immoral that wealthy people, because they could afford the best medical care, should automatically get it, while poor people, who couldn't afford it, somehow mattered less.

The dream of ending the disparity seemed far away, of course, but Farmer was trying, struggling, to make Cange into a medical oasis, to prove that equality was possible one day. His progress was fitful. Until he finally had a blood bank, a CT scanner, and other high-tech equipment at Zanmi Lasante, he was often faced with the dilemma of how to treat a patient who would have a good chance of recovery if he lived in Boston but in the central plateau faced certain death. The decision was clear to Farmer: if at all possible, fly the patient to Boston. But such a decision involved complexity and controversy.

In early 2000, an eleven- or twelve-year-old Haitian named John—it's often impossible to know someone's exact age in Haiti because in the central plateau few have official birth certificates—was brought to Zanmi Lasante by his mother. The two of them were all that remained of the immediate family. The boy had swelling in his neck, which at first glance indicated scrofula, or TB in his lymph nodes. However, the nodes in John's neck were much harder, and his white blood cell count much higher, than would have been the case in someone with TB. Farmer suspected some kind of cancer, but a diagnosis that would take only hours in Boston can take weeks when made between Haiti and Boston.

John's fragile health meant time was critical. Farmer enlisted the help of a Brigham doctor in her early thirties, Serena Koenig, who had previously arranged for a young Haitian with a congenital heart defect to be flown to the States for successful treatment. Serena now spent much of her free time working for PIH. To help John, she found an oncologist at Massachusetts General Hospital who would make a diagnosis without charging a fee. But first a tissue sample had to be provided, which required a tricky biopsy that Farmer delegated to a very competent Haitian surgeon in Mirebalais. The doctor agreed to come to Cange, negotiating the twelve-hour trip through mud and streams, for a fee of several thousand dollars, a large sum in Haiti. Farmer didn't argue. The surgery took hours.

Scheduled to fly to Boston the next morning, Farmer brought John's blood and tissue samples with him. Serena, who was already in Boston, met Farmer and rushed the samples to the oncologist at Mass General. They'd been placed in formaldehyde because Zanmi Lasante didn't have the equipment to preserve the specimens in frozen sections. The use of formaldehyde delayed the diagnosis by three days.

The news came back mixed. John had nasopharyngeal carcinoma, an extremely rare cancer that attacks the throat and nasal passages, but if the disease is caught early, 60 to 70 percent of patients can be cured. Only a handful of hospitals in the States had the right equipment and experience to deal with the cancer. Serena and Farmer agreed to try to get John to Boston. Because Farmer was so busy, Serena did almost all the work. She calculated that the hospital bill for John could run $100,000. She begged and cajoled for three weeks, and finally Mass General agreed to take the case for free.

There were others details to work out. Serena, with the help of a dear friend of Farmer's in Port-au-Prince—a small, quiet, usually smiling woman named Ti Fifi, whom Farmer affectionately called the "Haitian Godfather"—arranged for a fake birth certificate for John. That would get him a passport and visa to leave the country. Serena then convinced a Haitian American woman, Carole Smarth, a young resident at Mass General and the Brigham, to fly with her to Port-au-Prince. The plan was for them to accompany the boy back to Boston and Mass General. Because Carole spoke Creole, she would be able to comfort John on the journey.

Serena was afraid that in her absence the boy might have grown much sicker. She called Farmer, who was traveling, and asked what circumstances would keep them from bringing John to Boston.

"No circumstances," Farmer said. "It's his only chance."

"What will I say if I'm asked why we're doing this?"

"That his mother brought him to us," said Farmer. "And we're doing everything we can to help him."

I accompanied Carole and Serena on the flight from Boston to Port-au-Prince. Serena brought a suitcase full of stuffed animals and toys for the Cange pediatric ward. Carole carried a gigantic bag filled with medicines she thought they might need to get John safely through his trip. She also carried a plastic bag with water and goldfish for Farmer's pond at his Cange house (he'd asked for the favor, if it wasn't too much trouble, he said). The plan was to meet Ti Fifi and pick up John's travel documents in Port-au-Prince, drive in the Zanmi Lasante truck to Cange for the night, and fly the boy to Boston as soon as possible. Farmer was in Europe for a scientific meeting.

It was evening before we reached Cange. Carole, Serena, and Ti Fifi went right up to the Children's Pavilion. The sight of John in his bed shocked me. In photographs taken when he arrived a month earlier, he had looked merely sick. Now his legs and arms were so emaciated that I could see all the bones in them, and his knee and elbow joints looked outsize, with the flesh shrunk away. He'd been given a tracheotomy—a hole had been made in the front of his neck so a breathing tube could be inserted into his trachea, or windpipe. He also had a feeding tube fixed in the front of his neck, which pushed lumps of flesh to the sides. He was shifting around, clearly trying to find a way to take the pressure off his neck. He made a gurgling sound—secretions clogging his airways. A nurse was there to suction them out so he wouldn't suffocate. On top of everything else, he was running a fever. His eyes looked immense, like the eyes of a frightened woodland creature.

I couldn't look at him again right away. My gaze swam to John's mother, a dark-skinned, very thin woman who sat on the side of the bed, staring at nothing, it seemed. Carole leaned over John and spoke softly in Creole. "*Pa pe*—don't be afraid," she said, and tears began to roll down the boy's face.

A discussion followed between Ti Fifi and two Zanmi Lasante doctors about whether John was well enough to travel. Carole had purchased first-class tickets on a commercial flight, but now everyone worried that John's condition was so fragile, his appearance so scary, that the airline pilot might not allow them to fly. No one was even sure John could survive the wretched Highway 3 to reach Port-au-Prince. Even if they boarded the plane, Carole would have to take a suction device for John's neck—would using it disturb other passengers? They began to think about a helicopter to ferry them from Cange to Port-au-Prince, and then a special medevac flight straight to Boston. That would be the easiest, safest way, but the cost for both would be over $20,000. Serena said they should go ahead and pay it—and raise the money later—because not only might John die on the commercial flight, but also there might be no end of criticism of PIH for its reckless patient care. Serena began to feel responsible for making the boy wait so long for this moment, an entire month. Carole reminded her that a month ago they hadn't even had a diagnosis. Even so, Serena said, she should have brought him to Boston much earlier.

Serena emailed Farmer about her concerns, urging Paul to consider the medevac option. John still had a fighting chance, she said.

Farmer wrote back, "Serena, honey, please consider other options."

Serena and Ti Fifi tried to decipher the message. Paul wasn't exactly saying no to the medevac option, but they sensed he was growing concerned about the consequences of giving one patient special treatment while someone else in equally critical condition might not be allowed the same opportunity. A medevac flight was very rare, but expectations among patients would surely be raised. Why John when there were so many other cases?

Farmer was emailed again. Ti Fifi wrote that she needed him to be definitive. His reply came fairly quickly. "Well," he wrote of the cost of the medevac, "it could be worse. Getting him on the plane is the only way to save his life, so I'm for it." He added that he would be returning to Haiti within twenty-four hours.

The immediate challenge was to get John to Port-au-Prince. Serena and Ti Fifi had been unsuccessful in finding a helicopter or small plane to fly them. There was no manual suctioning device at Zanmi Lasante to take on the three-hour ride on Highway 3, should John's airway get clogged with secretions. They did have an electric suctioning device, but where and how would they charge it? Without it, John could suffocate. Ti Fifi got on the phone and hired a private ambulance company in Port-au-Prince—Sam's Service Ambulance—which owned a shiny old recycled ambulance from the 1970s. The proprietor, whose name wasn't Sam but Ralph, had served ten years in the U.S. Army and come home to make a modest living and in the process try to help his fellow Haitians. He and his three employees set out for Cange in a heavy rainstorm, while Carole, Serena, Ti Fifi, John, his mother, and I waited in a Zanmi Lasante truck, to meet them partway. At one point the streams that crossed Highway 3 became so swollen I worried they would engulf the ambulance. Twice Ralph called Ti Fifi on his cell phone to report that the ambulance had broken down—the engine tended to overheat when there wasn't enough motor oil. There were moments when no one was sure John would get to Port-au-Prince. But somehow Ralph always restarted the ambulance, and eventually we hooked up. Most important, in a day of improbable miracles, Ralph was able to connect the suctioning device to the ambulance's cigarette lighter and make John comfortable. Serena began to hope again. The medevac plane had been booked for the next day.

Everyone reached the airport on time and boarded the

small Learjet that took us to Boston. The team at the Mass General pediatric intensive care unit was waiting. John was quickly put in a bed and prepared for more tests. When Farmer called from Haiti, Serena said, "Hey, we did the *right* thing." Farmer was agreeing emphatically, I could tell, and Serena said again, "I have no doubt we did the right thing." When she spoke to the head of pediatrics, a small, trim middle-aged man in a black suit named Dr. Alan Ezekowitz, he smiled at Serena and said, "Well, this boy is a challenge. But I've cured sicker kids." She laughed nervously and said, "Well, now he's in Man's Greatest Hospital." That was what Mass General people called the place, playing off the initials MGH. There was a feeling of hope in the air.

The next afternoon Serena called me and said that a top group of radiologists, pediatricians, and cancer doctors had just spent an hour studying John's X-rays, bone scans, and CT scans. Then she began to weep. Her words came out as if all in one breath, "It's everywhere. It's in his mouth, it grows into the vertebral bodies. The poor kid has been in horrible pain. It started in the nasal area, just one solid tumor, growing back into the spinal column, the roof of the mouth. You can't radiate four vertebral bodies. So he's gonna die. He's getting excellent care, but there's still a bit of 'Why did you bring him? Why?'"

Serena's soul-searching led her through a series of questions and answers on the phone, directed at me, but she was really talking to herself, analyzing every step she'd taken, like someone who wanted to be doubly sure she'd done the right thing. She and Carole spent most of the next two weeks in John's room, taking turns sleeping there on a cot. He was no longer in pain thanks to proper medication. Sometimes he pretended to talk to his mother on a play phone, asking her to "come quick." He would motion for Carole to say the same words over the phone, and she did, and he was satisfied.

John's mother arrived within several days, along with Ti Fifi, who had made the arrangements for the mom. Farmer spent a great deal of time with John in his hospital room. The boy had many visitors, from PIH and from Boston's Haitian community, surrounding him with toys and smiles of love. After his death, there was talk that John might have lived if he could have left Haiti sooner, but almost everyone seemed grateful he'd gotten out at all. People said that at least his mother wouldn't have to grieve for her son in a room with flies on everyone's face.

John's death had unforeseen, consoling consequences. Farmer offered John's mother a job at Zanmi Lasante, and a large collection was taken up for her. Many had feared Farmer would be criticized for going to costly extremes to save one particular life, and that parents would besiege Zanmi Lasante with demands that their sick children be flown to Boston. The next time I was in Cange, however, I asked Zanmi Lasante's chief handyman, Ti Jean, what people were saying about the case. Ti Jean was a muscular man in his thirties, a local farmer's son who had witnessed what

Farmer had accomplished in the central plateau over the last twenty years. He told me that everyone talked about John and the medevac flight. "And you know what they say?" he confided. "They say, 'Look how much they care about us.'"

Serena had worried this might be the last time Mass General would give one of PIH's Haitian patients free care, but the pediatrics unit, especially its head, Dr. Ezekowitz, had warmed up to Serena and Carole, impressed by the compassion and attention they gave all their patients. Less than a month after John died, Serena flew from Haiti to Boston with another extremely sick child, this one well enough to fly commercially, and Mass General waived the cost of the little girl's care.

Farmer met Dr. Ezekowitz for the first time after John was admitted. The pediatrics chief already knew of Farmer's work and found it remarkable. It didn't take much convincing from Paul before Ezekowitz agreed that Mass General would treat several Haitian patients a year without charge. Ezekowitz told me later, "I think free care serves an important purpose, in that it centers people. Poverty in a place like Haiti is difficult to personalize. If it's in front of you, it has reality."

◆―◆―◆

Dr. Ezekowitz's statement was typical of the small victories that kept Farmer's spirits elevated and gave momentum to his mission. But my thoughts kept straying back to John. The incredible effort of moving the boy to Boston, then watching him die, later struck me as an object lesson in the difficulty of Farmer's mission, perhaps in its ultimate futility. I planned to ask him for his thoughts about the case, after a decent interval.

CHAPTER 28

───── ••• ─────

IN DECEMBER, TWO months after John's medevac flight
to Boston, I am back with Farmer in Haiti, as our truck's
headlights bounce over the endless, back-jarring potholes
of Highway 3. Farmer, eager to return to his clinic and patients, drives as fast as he can, as usual. We talk about how
his life is more hectic than ever—he now receives two hundred emails a day—yet he insists he can juggle the ever-
expanding load and that he isn't burned out. "It's still
doable," he tells me.

When we arrive in Cange, Ti Jean serves us dinner at
Farmer's house. Ti Jean, who has learned something about
medicine and gives a portion of his paycheck to destitute

patients, is also Paul's main local male confidant—"my chief of staff," Farmer calls him. He looks after Paul as closely as he tends to the grounds and the buildings of Zanmi Lasante.

Ti Jean is also one of Farmer's chief informants on local beliefs.

"See that black dog, Polo? Was it here yesterday?"

"No."

"And did it bark twice?"

"Yes."

Ti Jean will nod knowingly. "Mmm-hmmm."

In his worldview, as Farmer understands it, people turn themselves into animals for shifty reasons, or else local sorcerers turn them into animals as punishment, or simply for food. Farmer listens good-naturedly, interpreting Ti Jean's words as "a giant morality play, a commentary on social inequality."

After our dinner we gaze into the lit pond outside the house. The pair of fish that Carole brought from Boston are now swimming happily among the others, and Farmer names the species for me. Though the fish are expensive to maintain, Ti Jean looks upon the pond approvingly because he knows it makes Farmer happy. "If you only saw patients," he says, "you might not be happy."

What about all his travel? Farmer asks him.

Ti Jean allows that Farmer travels a lot. "You're like a restless bird," he says.

"Where *is* my nest?" Farmer asks.

"Your nest is Haiti," says Ti Jean. "You go everywhere, but this is your base."

————◆◆◆◆————

Some months back, a small, trusting thirteen-year-old boy with shiny dark eyes, named Alcante, had arrived at Zanmi Lasante's Children's Pavilion. Like John, he had lumps on his neck, but in Alcante's case they were in fact symptomatic of scrofula. First-line antibiotics wiped out the infection, and he recovered with only a few scars left on his neck. Alcante had such a beautiful presence that he seemed like the guardian angel of the pavilion, but Farmer worried about what would happen when he returned to his home in the central plateau. Other family members were most likely the carriers of the bacteria that had infected him. Farmer sent the clinic's community health workers to bring them all to Zanmi Lasante. Several had TB, including Alcante's father, who is still in therapy. Now Farmer plans to hike to their homestead, in a tiny town called Casse, to check on the family.

The hike is supposed to be longer than the first one I took with Farmer to Morne Michel, though not as steep, but after we set out I'm imagining a very long day. I'm sure of it when Ti Jean, who is accompanying us along with the clinic's pharmacist, asks if I've brought my flashlight. I haven't and offer to go back for it. Farmer waves me off. Everything will be fine, he insists, and besides, he can't go back: there will be some urgent situation he won't be able to turn down and thus he will be further delayed. He is wearing a baseball cap, and as he pushes ahead, looking very much like a determined leader, I realize I'm not worried about the flashlight. This strikes me as unusual. I've never found it easy to trust another person to lead me anywhere, but I trust Farmer.

We head off along dirt paths etched into the sides of the hills beside the Pèligre reservoir, and soon I'm scrambling up the eroded face of a cliff. I'm soaked in sweat by the time we get to the top, where Farmer is waiting for me, just like on our epic hike to Morne Michel. I take a long swig of my filtered water—Farmer and Ti Jean haven't drunk anything yet—as we stride across a ridge through yellow grass. Farmer points out "the peculiarly steep and conical hill" on which he sat in solitude years ago, writing *AIDS and Accusation*.

On the way to Casse we make a house call, stopping at a hut to greet an elderly-looking couple sitting together on a straw mat. Farmer has brought along the man's medical records. He suffers from hypertension and was also seen at the clinic for malaria. Despite instructions to return for a checkup, he didn't reappear. Farmer kneels on the dirt floor and takes the man's pulse and blood pressure, then puts a stethoscope to his chest. The air inside the hut is still and hot, vibrating with flies. Several small children have come to the doorway to peer in.

Farmer says to them, speaking of the old woman in the

house, "You love her a lot? Do you tell her? Don't lie to me now." The children giggle. The old woman smiles.

The man's blood pressure is too high. He also complains of chest pains and weakness in his legs. Farmer suspects he's had a stroke because he has difficulty walking. It would be most helpful to have a pair of Canadian crutches—forearm crutches, not underarm ones—to help stabilize his walk, but this means someone has to make another trip from the clinic. If we were at the Brigham, Farmer says, this would all be easy to manage, including physical therapy for the man. Farmer takes the wife's blood pressure, too, at her request—her numbers are high as well. He gives the couple some pills and instructions.

As we linger—goodbyes are always long in Haiti—I feel a vague pain in my chest; it's been on and off since our first cliff climb. I apologize when I tell Farmer because I'm sure it's nothing, but he asks me a dozen questions and concludes it's probably just heartburn. I'm supposed to tell him if it gets worse.

"Is there a long way still to go?" I ask as we finally move on.

"Oh, yeah! This is a quarter of the way there."

"A quarter?"

The day is ferociously warm. Farmer hasn't drunk any water yet. I have plenty of time to think as we trudge on. Since the death of John, I've been trying to form my question about his case. I remember a remark Farmer made to me a year ago in these hills: "You *should* compare suffering. Which suffering is worse. It's called triage."

He was referring to a situation where you have more than one person in need of serious medical attention, but your resources are too limited to treat them both. So you choose one patient over another. This could mean one of two things. In warfare, for example, you attend first to the severely wounded who have the best chance of survival. The aim is to save as many as possible; the others may have to die unattended. In peacetime, however, in a well-staffed, well-stocked American emergency room, triage isn't about withholding care from anyone; rather, it's identifying the patients in the gravest danger and treating them first. The ultimate goal is to save everyone.

Farmer has constructed his life around this second kind of triage. What else is a preferential option for the poor in medicine? But Haiti more nearly resembles a battlefield than a place at peace.

Walking behind Farmer, I finally bring up John. Not long after he died, a relatively new PIH-er said to me that she couldn't help thinking of all the things they could have done with that $20,000. As I tell Farmer this, I quickly add, "I don't mean this at all critically."

"Come on," he says over his shoulder. "I'm not hyper-sensitive. But we've already discussed this, so many times."

I don't want to upset him, but I recognize his tone. He's just delivering a preamble.

"Let me say a couple of things about this particular case," he continues, talking over his shoulder to me as we walk on. "One is to remember, of course, that John was referred to Boston as dying of a treatable tumor, a very rare tumor. He wasn't referred to Mass General before we knew what we had. So when he was referred, it was for free care because it was such a rare thing and it was treatable. That was what the decision was made on. And there was no way for us to find out that John didn't have locally invasive disease because it requires a diagnostic test that we can't do here. So the bottom line is, why do we intervene as aggressively as we can with that kid and not with another? Because his mother brought him to us and that's where he was, in our clinic."

I wondered whether, if Farmer had been at the clinic to see how emaciated John was, to see him in the condition in which I saw him, he would have agreed with Carole and Serena to fly him to Boston. So I ask him.

"The emaciation wouldn't have stopped me," he says. "If I'd seen how far he'd gone downhill, I wouldn't have stopped the process. Why? On what grounds? We didn't know until he got to Boston that the cancer had invaded the vertebrae."

We climb another cliff, and I am breathing too hard to speak. After a pause, Farmer says he's a little troubled by the new PIH-er's comments, because he has to *work* with these people. "The last thing I want to do is expend my energy trying to convince my own coworkers."

"I don't want to misrepresent it," I say. "Your PIH-er wasn't saying you shouldn't have brought John to Boston. Only that it was a shame you had to spend so much, given what else you could do with twenty grand."

"Yeah, but there are so many ways of saying that," he replies. "For example, why didn't the airline company pay for the flight? That's a way of saying it. Or how about this way? How about if I say I have fought for *my whole life* a long defeat. How about that? How about if I said, 'That's all it adds up to is defeat'?"

"A long defeat."

"I have fought the long defeat and brought other people on to fight the long defeat, and I'm not going to stop because we keep losing. Now I actually think sometimes we may *win*. I don't dislike victory. You and I have discussed this so many times."

"Sorry."

"No, I'm not complaining," he says. "You know, people from my background—like you, like most PIH-ers, like me—we're used to being on a victory team, and actually what we're really trying to do in PIH is to make common cause with the *losers*. Those are two very different things. We want to be on the winning team, but at the risk of turning our backs on the losers, no, it's not worth it. So you fight the long defeat."

I tell him that I like the line about the long defeat.

"I would regard that as the basic stance of O for the P,"

he says. "I don't care if we lose, I'm gonna try to do the right thing."

"But you're going to try to win."

"Of course!"

After we scramble down a hilly section of the trail, he asks how my chest is. It feels all right, in fact. Farmer goes back to our subject. "If we could identify losers like John, and not waste our energy and time on them, then we'd all be good, as they say in the States. Right? But the point of O for the P is that you never do that. Because before you turn your back on someone like John you have to be really sure, and the more you learn about John's family the more you realize he was the last kid. They're extinct. His mother's bloodline is just gone. It sounds Darwinian, but you know what I mean. How can you be an O for the P doc and be willing to take that risk without all the data you can get?"

We have been trudging through deep country, far from any road, and yet there's hardly been a moment when other people haven't been in sight or just around the next turn in the trail. Many are patients of Zanmi Lasante and greet Farmer and Ti Jean warmly. We've been walking now for at least four hours. I am virtually out of water, but the water Ti Jean and Farmer are carrying is unfiltered—they have both built up an immunity to local microorganisms—so they advise me not to drink it.

"We getting close to Casse?" I ask.

"Well, you don't want to know just yet." Farmer smiles

and points to a hilltop in the distance. "Wait'll we get over that ridge. Then I'll break it to you."

My mouth has grown so dry that I croak when I try to speak. Farmer has noticed and finds some oranges at a farmyard. I consume six in a row, sitting with my back against a tree. When we finally reach Casse, a brown and dusty, dirt-street market town made of wood and corrugated metal, Farmer feeds me Cokes. I tell him I feel much better.

"Hydration," he says.

Zanmi Lasante's local health worker—a barefoot woman in a dress—shows us the way to Alcante's farm. It's a half-hour walk to a hut made of mud and sticks, a cook shack with a fireplace, and a field of millet. As we approach the abode, it looks forlorn and dismal. "On a scale of one to ten," Farmer tells me, "this is a one."

Suddenly we're greeted by a shiny little boy. "Alcante!" says Farmer. "I'm happy to see you."

The boy calls to his sisters, who emerge from the hut along with the rest of the family. I'm reminded of the circus routine in which an apparently endless stream of clowns comes out of a tiny car. I count ten souls who live in the hut. Alcante looks for chairs for everyone.

Greetings are exchanged, and Farmer checks everyone with his stethoscope. He tells me how TB is such a deceptive disease; it doesn't always reveal itself by a sputum culture, as it did for the father. Most of Alcante's family has or had extrapulmonary TB, which is much harder to detect until it begins to spread, and then it can be fatal. It seems so unfair that a whole family like this is struck by one disease, Farmer laments.

"Are you going to punish people for thinking TB comes from sorcery?" he says. Farmer reminds me of the woman who asked him years ago, "Are you incapable of complexity?" And once again I see his point that life in Haiti can be so dreadful that if you live and suffer here, you have to look for multiple explanations for the unbearable.

He concludes the dismount, saying he's glad we came, so that we could know how necessary it is to intervene aggressively.

I know what this means: a new house with a concrete floor and metal roof for the family, an effort to improve their nutrition, school tuition for the kids. The Farmer method: first you cure the family of TB, then you change the conditions that made them vulnerable to the disease. I am aware that his critics would say Farmer just spent seven hours on two house calls when he could have been making an important speech to an important health organization, impacting the hearts and minds of influential people. But Farmer likes being grounded in the kind of obscurity, away from the media and spotlight, that refreshes his passion and authority; doctoring to the poor is his ultimate source of power. There's also a very practical reason for clambering up and down mountains, or doing anything arduous and unglamorous, what PIH-ers called "scut work." In public health projects in difficult locales, theory often prevails over practice. Individual patients get forgotten, and what seems like a small problem gets ignored until it grows large, like MDR. "If you focus on individual patients," Jim Kim says, "you can't get sloppy."

Farmer knows he will always have his critics with their notions about efficiency, about cost-effectiveness, about how PIH and Zanmi Lasante will crumble and fold without Jim or Paul to keep them alive. He doesn't seem to worry about it. Earlier today he said that he'd brought on others to fight "the long defeat." The numbers are impressive. They include priests and nuns and professors and secretaries and businessmen and church ladies and peasants like Ti Jean and also dozens of medical students and doctors who have enlisted to work in places such as Cange and Siberia and the slums of Lima, often with little or no pay. I once heard Farmer say that he hoped a day would come when he could do a good job just by showing up. It seemed to me that time has already arrived. A great deal of what he's started goes on without him now.

After saying goodbye to Alcante's family, we reach Casse around dusk. Since I'm without a flashlight, Farmer and Ti Jean decide to take a different route than the way we came— one without rivers to cross and steep cliffs to scramble down. I think they don't believe I'd make it. My pride is hurt, but I'm secretly relieved. Farmer stops a young man on a motorbike and asks if he'd give one of our party, the pharmacist, a lift to Cange. The man says yes, but he wants a hundred dollars. Then he recognizes Doktè Paul and he's not so insistent on his price after Farmer points out, "And if you get sick, I won't ask you for a hundred dollars." He accepts Farmer's offer to pay for his gas, and when he reaches Cange he will send a truck for Ti Jean, Farmer, and me. In the meantime, because Farmer feels like walking some more, we begin marching along a dirt road, the route the truck will have to take.

The light is fading now and gray clouds billow over the mountains we crossed earlier. Soon, with complete darkness, the stars pop out. "This is nice," Farmer says. A cozy feeling seems to spread from him. It's as if we're three kids out after bedtime and we can say whatever is really on our minds but don't have to. I sing a line of a marching song I learned when I served with the U.S. Army in the Vietnam War: "You had a good home but you left."

"You had a good bus but you left," sings Farmer.

Roosters crow in the night. Now and then a dog barks. In the next few minutes several different parties of men pass us silently. Farmer says *"Bonsoir"* to one man and Ti Jean shushes him, then issues these instructions: if someone passes you at night and doesn't speak, you, too, must remain silent, but if the person asks who you are, you must say, "I am who you are," and if the person asks what you do, you must say, "I do what you do."

"What's the danger?" Farmer asks.

Ti Jean says you might be talking to a demon who will steal your spirit. Then you'll wake up in the morning very sick, and a doctor will say you have typhoid or malaria, but in fact the problem will be more complex. "You should take the medicines," says Ti Jean. "But then you should also go to a Voodoo priest." The fact is, Ti Jean explains, that three-quarters of all Voodoo ceremonies are an effort to drive away illness, not to put a curse on someone.

We've walked three hours from Casse, eleven hours in all today, when I finally feel I can't go any farther. I tell Farmer, and I'm grateful that he doesn't tease me. We all stop to rest on the side of the lumpy dirt road. I pull out a candy bar for the three of us to share as we gaze at a radio tower across the border in the Dominican Republic. Farmer's gentle doctor's voice comes from behind me, asking how I feel. I tell him the truth—I'm tired but fine. And then, with him having seen his last patient of the day, as if now he can finally relax, his long, lean frame sinks back into the ground, his eyes searching the sky. "There's Orion's belt. . . ."

From somewhere in the valley below comes the sound of drums. I suddenly recall the sound of Voodoo drums wafting into the army barracks in Mirebalais at night, when I visited Haiti as a journalist, around the time I first met Farmer. I remember how unsettling it was to some of us there, in all its mystery. I'm sure we'd have felt differently if we had thought we were hearing ceremonies to cure the sick. For myself, right now, I like the sound, like so many hearts beating through a single stethoscope.

POSTSCRIPT: HAITI NOW

IN JUNE 2002, seven years after the death of Father Jack Roussin, the World Health Organization adopted new guidelines for treating MDR-TB, virtually the same as Partners in Health had successfully used in Peru. For Jim Kim, this marked a victory in the long campaign to push down the price of second-line TB treatment and make it available to poor countries everywhere. In the last ten years, however, less than 1 percent of the roughly 5 million people who developed MDR had access to appropriate treatment, and 1.5 million died, according to a 2011 report from Médecins Sans Frontières (Doctors Without Borders). There were several reasons for this setback. TB programs in developing nations are generally underfunded, resulting in weak delivery systems for treatment and prevention. Inaccurate data from countries with high incidences of MDR have made it difficult for pharmaceutical companies to meet demand for these drugs consistently, and therefore market prices have fluctuated. Finally, pharmaceutical companies have sometimes had limited access to quality ingredients. For now, the cost of treating MDR-TB is approximately 475 times greater than treating first-line TB, according to PIH.

One bright spot in the war on MDR has been Socios en Salud's work in Peru. What Jim Kim and Jaime Bayona started in the slums of Carabayllo has been expanded to sixteen rural health posts, where an increasing number of MDR patients are successfully treated. In collaboration with the Peruvian Ministry of Health, Socios also started an MDR clinic in Arequipa, the country's second-most-populous city. Today, Peru boasts the highest cure rate for MDR in the world. Socios en Salud continues to support nearly fifteen hundred MDR patients, as well as provide clinical, nutritional, and psychological support for more than a thousand people living with or affected by HIV and AIDS. In 2008, Jaime Bayona left Socios en Salud to become the director of global health programs and practice for the Dartmouth Center for Health Care Delivery Science.

The last ten years have seen steady progress in the fight against HIV/AIDS. Since its inception in 2002, the Global Fund to Fight AIDS, TB, and Malaria has spent $22.6 billion for more than a thousand programs in 150 countries, including funding PIH and other health organizations in Haiti, Russia, Peru, and Rwanda. Global Fund, which has become one of the world's main private financiers in the fight against infectious diseases, reports that to date anti-retroviral therapy has been provided for 3.3 million HIV/AIDS patients, 8.6 million people have received some form of TB treatment, and 230 million insecticide-treated mosquito nets have been made available in malaria-infested areas. With the advance in HIV/AIDS treatment protocols, the disease has been transformed from a certain death sentence to a manageable chronic illness—but only for those with access to treatment. Malaria continues to claim more lives than any other disease, with some health organizations estimating up to 2 million deaths a year. In 2010, 8.8 million people fell ill with TB, with 1.4 million deaths. Ninety-five percent of cases reported were in the developing world.

Partners in Health continues to play a significant role in global health. Ophelia Dahl, executive director of PIH, now oversees an organization of fifteen thousand people: doctors, nurses, administrators, researchers, lab technicians, mental health workers, social workers, community health workers, procurement specialists, fund-raisers, a public relations and social media staff, and a communications and development group. PIH maintains a foothold in ten countries—Peru, Kazakhstan, Mexico, Dominican Republic, Rwanda, Malawi, Lesotho, Russia, Haiti, and the United States. Like-minded organizations—some with the help of PIH—have sprung up in Asia and other parts of the world. Learning from its lessons in Peru, Haiti, and Russia, PIH works closely with governments and their agencies to minimize political misunderstandings and to deploy their complementary resources. New programs to treat cancer and other chronic diseases are growing. The strongest push continues to be into rural areas, where the need for clean water, schools, employment, and housing is interrelated with health care.

PIH's core mission has never deviated from what it was

when Jim, Paul, and Ophelia first met to discuss how to change the world's approach to health care. However, strategies have evolved, including lobbying efforts in Washington, D.C., as the global economic crisis has diminished public funding. Corporate sponsors, green technology partners, and microfinance nonprofits have helped fill the funding gap, and individual contributions are more important than ever. PIH works closely with Harvard Medical School and the Brigham and Women's Hospital, and through their collaborative initiatives, a new generation of doctors and health specialists have chosen careers centered on infectious diseases. And through Twitter, Facebook, and PIH's own website, when new health and humanitarian crises occur, such as the January 2010 earthquake and the 2010–2012 cholera outbreak in Haiti, the response can be instantaneous.

The 7.0-magnitude earthquake and its fifty-two aftershocks killed an estimated 316,000 Haitians, injured 300,000, and instantly made more than a million people homeless. Donations to PIH helped provide medical assistance for victims both in Port-au-Prince, which was near the earthquake's epicenter, and at the Zanmi Lasante facilities in the central plateau and the lower Artibonite Valley. PIH brought in engineering teams to stabilize the capital's badly damaged general hospital, restoring its water and electricity; when medical supplies were trucked in, twelve operating rooms were quickly up and running.

Many lives were saved, but months passed before anyone felt the worst was over; protecting property, restoring sanitation facilities, building temporary shelters, and supplying food and clean water were constant challenges. If there was a silver lining, it was that the earthquake brought new funding and world attention to a country that had suffered in obscurity through too many natural, political, and health disasters. As Port-au-Prince and other cities were rebuilt, new housing, schools, and health projects were initiated. This included a 320-bed teaching hospital, Mirebalais National Teaching Hospital, to educate the next generation of Haitian medical students.

The PIH response to the cholera epidemic was equally swift. Cholera is an acute diarrheal disease caused by consuming water or food contaminated with a particular type of bacteria; it can be fatal if a victim is not treated with fluids within hours of becoming sick. The latest outbreak was allegedly the result of human waste contaminating a local water supply in the central plateau. Within a month the disease had spread into almost every province of Haiti, including Port-au-Prince, as well as the neighboring Dominican Republic. As alerts came through email, texts, and phone calls, medical teams from Zanmi Lasante partnered with other international nongovernmental organizations (NGOs), their staff members walking up to six hours a day to set up hydration posts in distant villages. The Mirebalais cholera center was overwhelmed. By January 2012, more then seven thousand deaths from cholera had been reported, and thousands of people were hospitalized. The effort to step up cholera vaccinations has been steady but inadequate. While forty thousand people have been vaccinated since the epidemic began, the ultimate goal is to inoculate a hundred thousand Haitians. Experts believe that cholera will continue to spike and ebb in Haiti until safe public water systems are available throughout the country.

When responding to disasters, one challenge for PIH and all other NGOs has been to direct as much funding as possible into on-the-ground projects. After the Haitian earthquake, hopes of quickly rebuilding the country were frustrated by a lack of control over money. Too much went to pay overhead—consultants, intermediaries, transportation companies, government fees—and not enough reached those in need. PIH staff has begun to focus on methods of structuring aid and loans so that in the future the sick and indigent will be the primary beneficiaries.

The work that Farmer started in Haiti more than thirty years ago continues to evolve. Today PIH runs eleven clinics and hospitals, and it provides jobs for more than 5,400 Haitians—doctors, nurses, lab technicians, pharmacists, and counselors. The result is that communities get both health care and badly needed income. The clinic in Cange no longer has to rely solely on a generator for power; with a petition to President Aristide from Ti Fifi and other Cangeois, electricity finally came to Zanmi Lasante from the dam turbines at Péligre. The clinic provides its patients with state-of-the-art medical technology, including a blood bank that serves much of the central plateau, and a sophisticated lab. Instead of having to be flown to Boston for diagnosis and treatment, a patient like John, for whom Serena, Carole, and Ti Fifi moved heaven and earth in an effort to save his life, in most cases can now be treated in Haiti.

Farmer continues to consult with Haitian doctors in Zanmi Lasante, but most of his clinic work is in Rwanda, where he lives with Didi and two of their three children. Catherine, whose second birthday I celebrated with Farmer and Didi in their Paris apartment, is a teenager and attends a boarding school in the United States. Farmer's travel schedule, like his emails and texts, offers no promise of subsiding. He continues to lecture, attend meetings and conferences, treat patients, and raise funds for PIH. In 2009, he accepted a position as United Nations deputy special envoy for Haiti, working closely with United Nations Special Envoy for Haiti Bill Clinton. He also began working with the Clinton Global Initiative, a foundation started by the former president to bring together experts and leaders to find solutions to major world problems.

In 2003, Jim Kim, like Farmer ten years earlier, was awarded a MacArthur "genius" grant. In the same year, while remaining on the PIH board of directors, he joined WHO as an adviser to the director-general. A year later he became director of WHO's HIV/AIDS department, focusing on initiatives to help poor countries scale up their treatment, prevention, and care programs. Unlike MDR antibiotics, prices of antiretroviral drugs have continued to fall, and WHO assisted in the treatment of up to seven million Africans with HIV and AIDS—and millions more in Asia, Eastern Europe, and Latin America. Jim also served as a Harvard professor in medicine and was chair of its Department of Global Health and Social Medicine. In March 2009, he left WHO and Harvard to become the seventeenth president of Dartmouth—the first Asian American president of any Ivy League university. In March 2012, President Obama nominated him to be president of the World Bank, a post to which he won election three months later.

Père Lafontant continues to work in the central plateau and remains a close friend of Farmer and Kim. Tom White died in January 2011, but not before realizing his ambition to give away virtually every last dollar to philanthropy. A Christmas 2010 note accompanied his final check to PIH. "Dear Ophelia," he wrote, "Approximately thirty years ago, when joining with you, Paul, Jim and Todd, I received a tremendous gift. For the first time in my life, I was able to give with complete confidence that my donations would be used in the best possible way. Peace, light, love, happiness to all of you extraordinary people."

TRACY KIDDER graduated from Harvard University and studied at the University of Iowa. He has won the Pulitzer Prize, the National Book Award, the Robert F. Kennedy Award, and many other literary prizes. The author of *My Detachment, Mountains Beyond Mountains, Home Town, Old Friends, Among Schoolchildren, House,* and *The Soul of a New Machine,* Kidder lives in Massachusetts and Maine.

———— ·◄ ►· ————

MICHAEL FRENCH, a graduate of Stanford University, is the author of twenty-two books, including biographies, art criticism, and fiction for adults and young adults. He has adapted many acclaimed works for young people. French divides his time between Santa Barbara, California, and Santa Fe, New Mexico.